Physical Therapy

THE TRUTH

For Students, Clinicians, and
Healthcare Professionals

MONIE PHILLIPS, PT

Bloomington, IN Milton Keynes, UK

authorHOUSE

AuthorHouse™
1663 Liberty Drive, Suite 200
Bloomington, IN 47403
www.authorhouse.com
Phone: 1-800-839-8640

AuthorHouse™ UK Ltd.
500 Avebury Boulevard
Central Milton Keynes, MK9 2BE
www.authorhouse.co.uk
Phone: 08001974150

First published by AuthorHouse 4/6/2006

ISBN: 1-4259-2464-6 (sc)

Library of Congress Control Number: 2006902098

Printed in the United States of America
Bloomington, Indiana

This book is printed on acid-free paper.

CONTENTS

INTRODUCTION

If you are thinking about going into the field of physical therapy, or if you have recently completed the physical therapy program, this book is for you. If you are a seasoned professional, this book may bring you comfort in knowing you are not alone in your daily struggles. I graduated from the PT program in 1996, and I realized quickly that the actual practice of the art was the least of my worries. When I started my first job, the billing and the politics of the business demanded my immediate attention. Years later I realized that it would have been helpful to know something about these issues prior to applying for my first job. I could have made a much better decision if I would have been educated in some of the unspoken rules. It is my hope that this book will inform you of some of the positive and negative aspects of the healthcare arena, before you get into the field. I am a licensed physical therapist currently working in an acute-care hospital setting as the director of rehabilitation services.

I have experience in most healthcare settings, excluding pediatric care and the professional sports industry.

I would like to express to you that monetary gain and job satisfaction do not always go hand in hand. If you do not balance your motives, you will not be successful. If you get into PT for the money, it will not be long before you become disgruntled with the field and resentful of your choices. You will add to the existing healthcare problems or quit the field altogether within the first five years. You will not provide quality, objective therapy or put up with the daily challenges (and there are many) you will be faced with. Unless you are truly dedicated to the science, you will be miserable in the healthcare arena. Don't get me wrong. Therapists who love what they do are out there practicing, and they like the money but find it hard, because money tends to persuade people to do things that are ethically questionable. It is my opinion that, if money is the major factor on the professional's mind, the objectivity will not be one hundred percent, and that therapist is not what I would call dedicated to the profession. The world is watching, and when substandard therapy services delivered by unethical therapists makes the mainstream news, the field of physical therapy will suffer the consequences. Therefore, make sure you are interested in the science before you commit.

The greatest challenges I faced in many different settings had to do with billing and the political end of the business—not the actual science of physical therapy and the application of its principles to patient care. Worrying about how to practice physical therapy was a great concern of mine when I graduated college. I felt I would not have enough knowledge or clinical experience, but I was wrong. College prepared me for hands-on application and drilled the knowledge in so deeply that therapy was the easiest part. Dealing with the business end and the politics was an altogether new adversary. I am not trying to imply that the professors did not discuss or teach some of these issues. They did. But my ability to comprehend was minimal, and the time they had to cover the material was not sufficient. I remember concentrating on the science during college, not the rules and regulations of Medicare or the state practice act. You will have to experience them firsthand to understand the dynamics behind the business and politics and how they relate to the professions ethics. But with this book, you should be more prepared to deal with these issues. It is my intention that this book will shed light on the issues of a person contemplating PT as a career. It is also my hope that PT graduates may gain insight into the daily struggles therapists are dealing with today and prepare for their practice with knowledge that will advance their ability to maintain the highest ethical principles. I would like to think that this book could be a comfort to the veteran PT as well. I would like to add that this profession is not alone in its dilemmas. All professional and non-professional careers face off daily with politics and money. Moral and ethical issues abound in all facets of the workforce, so please do not think that PT is alone in this.

Throughout the book, you will find that every principle points to the importance of abiding by the state practice act and Medicare rules and regulations. The reason it is important to know this is directly related to objectivity. The rules and regulations provided by the government and the state regarding the practice and payment for services rendered are there for a reason. Medicare and all of the private insurance companies are no different than you in regard to paying for services. We demand that our car be serviced properly by the local mechanic.

- Objectivity: Show me what is wrong and explain it in terms I can understand.

- Efficiency: I need my car back as soon as possible.

- Billing: Don't expect me to pay for something that does not work or something you did not do.

Most of the time, we walk away from these situations wondering, Did they stick it to me? Did they really change the right part? Was changing that part the most cost-effective solution? How long will it be before it brakes again?

Going into the healthcare field, we often think that people will trust us because we deal with helping people. But working on a car helps people, right? Once you graduate and begin to practice, be prepared to justify what you are doing. Providing patient care that is ethical, objective, and goal-based is the key to the future survival of our profession. Terms like *error rate testing* and *evidence-based strategies* are just two of the terms Medicare uses to refer to looking for over-utilization and improper billing. Medicare is preparing for the largest group of people in our nation to require medical assistance, and it is trying to accomplish this task by making sure healthcare professionals are providing the most efficient, cost-effective treatments available. It is my belief that this book will help the future physical therapist and the seasoned therapist accomplish that goal.

HEALTHCARE IN FLUX MODE

In the last ten years, the healthcare industry and the profession of physical therapy has witnessed change many times over, but the biggest change is yet to come and that is the compression of morbidity. The elderly population in this nation is rising to proportions that cannot be overlooked. If you are thinking of going into the field of health-related science, the information contained in this book will provide you with vital information that will affect your future. The information contained in this book will shed light on many facets of the healthcare industry. The billing side is very important, however, the politics on all levels plays a large role in healthcare as well, and it will affect your job in a gigantic way. The current shortage of nurses is something you probably never thought about, but this in and of itself will truly be one of the biggest components in the healthcare professional's future career satisfaction in settings that depend on nursing services. When the nursing staff is not happy in the hospital setting, no one is happy. Physical therapy, respiratory therapy, and other professions were conceived and nurtured by nurses, and when the shortage is at its worst, you will feel the pressure. Many articles today report that women are going into more lucrative professions with much lower stress thresholds. That includes people who were thinking about going into nursing. Nurses are in demand, but the money is not worth the stress load and the crazy hours. When you compare that to teaching, you can see why there is a shortage. I can remember when I had an airframe and power-plant license; I worked for seven dollars an hour on aircraft at a small airport. Someone told me that people working on sewing machines were making more money without having to document everything they did. Nor did they have to worry about the liability of killing people because of mechanical errors. I went into the aircraft industry for the wrong reasons, and that was a long time ago. My motives were not clear, and I got out of it because I did not have a passion to stay and put up with the problems associated with the job. That is why it is so important that you be prepared now, before you go into a field that will have problems. You will not be content if you are not truly passionate about the science.

Only a few people discover their passion, and fewer than that choose a profession they are passionate about. More people today find passion in monetary gain alone and the things they can buy with it. They also find themselves in situations that involve fraud, abuse, and the accompanying headaches from the stress of living a lie.

I will try to express the things that I feel you will need to be prepared for in a way that will not bias your opinion.

I hope to provide information that will shed light on your career choice and help you make the appropriate decision. I will briefly touch on college pre-requisite courses and provide a view of the actual physical therapy program. I will not be able to go course-by-course or get into the guts of it, but I will try to explain what it will take to get into the program and make it through with a satisfactory or better performance.

CAREER EXERCISE

A good exercise to help decide your career involves writing down what you are passionate about. Make sure to look at your hobbies and never let the amount of money or what type of lifestyle you would like influence your decision. Figure out what you would like to do for eight hours a day to be happy, if the job only pays room and board. If you can determine what would satisfy your soul in this way, I promise you will be successful in both job satisfaction, monetary gain, and life in general. If money seems to be the only thought in your head, think of what you need that money will buy to make you happy. If you determine that shelter, food, clothing, and safety are among these things then think harder because you probably already have these things. If you feel that money will resolve some problem in your life, ask the question, How will it make me feel better? Also, ask yourself if you would be willing to sacrifice your happiness for the money. If you chose a profession that you are not happy with, it will take away from your happiness and eventually destroy it. If you think hard enough about this issue, you will determine that having money to buy things that you think will make you happy has to be the biggest lie out there today. This story will help. I heard this story some time ago that influenced my life in a positive way and I think it is appropriate here.

Jane was the vice president of a large firm; she was very successful at her job. She made $250,000 a year, and she was very good at what she did. However, doing a good job and making a lot of money did not make her happy. She soon began experiencing health problems and found herself having a difficult time getting to sleep due to work-related stress. Jane decided that her health was most important, and she decided to quit her high-pressure, high-paying job. She knew she would have to sacrifice material things but it did not matter anymore. Her health was more important. She relaxed for a few months and collected her thoughts. She realized that she could start doing some of the things that made her happy, like making crafts. She had always enjoyed that and was quite good at it. She was passionate about this work and before long started a little business selling crafts. It was not long before she developed international contacts and began selling her products all over the world. Today she has a company that makes millions each year, and she is happy with what she does. Her stress level is at an all-time low and her health is great. When she looks back at all the time she spent going to college and all the time she wasted at the firm stressing over things that meant nothing to her, she thinks about what it would have been like if she would have followed her passion for crafts long ago. Now, I know you may be thinking that her experience as a vice president for a large successful firm had something to do with the success she experienced with crafts, and it could have. But for the sake of this example, forget it. The lesson is to follow your dreams, your passion.

Instead of going through the pain and suffering of learning this lesson ten or twenty years to late, follow your passion it will always lead to success. Having to make a decision to give all of what you have worked for to follow your dreams is a difficult task, and many are not willing to take the risk once they have dedicated a large part of their lives to their current professions. On top of it, you will more than likely have a family to support by then so it will be more difficult to start over due to the increased responsibility. Start with what you are passionate about first, and I know you will be successful. If you do not become a millionaire, I am sure that you will survive and I am positive you will be happy.

IMPROVE YOUR CHANCES OF GETTING INTO A PHYSICAL THERAPY PROGRAM

PREREQUISITES. GPA, AND INTERVIEW

Your college counselor can provide you with the correct prerequisite information, or you can visit a college with a physical therapy program and ask for it. I went straight to the source and requested the information. Besides, my college counselor advised me to go into something else. She said physical therapy was extremely hard to get into. I did not listen to her and I got in on the first try. Going to the physical therapy program department and asking questions can be good because you may meet some of the people on the selection board, and it proves you are interested in getting all the information you can to make the correct decision. This can make the interview process easier because you will feel more at ease, having already met the interviewers. It kind of breaks the ice and puts the interview process in a more relaxed mood. I went to the department several times, asking questions. I did not wear out my welcome, so whatever you do, please do not camp out at the department.

Once you have the prerequisite information, schedule your classes by grouping the more difficult classes with one easy class, and choose the professors who are known to be difficult. I know this does not seem right at this point in time. You're probably thinking you will not make a good grade and will lower your GPA, making it impossible to get in. But I am telling you the truth. Taking this path paid off for me. I took zoology, anatomy, and physiology with the hardest professor at my college. When I got into PT school and started gross anatomy and physiology, I did not struggle. I had a great base, and it helped more than you will ever know. I can remember thinking how easy the classes were, and I made a mental note to thank my zoology professor.

The physical therapy selection board looks at your grade point average, but that is not all. The board needs to make sure you can handle a load of hard classes. If you get into the program, they are not going to group gross anatomy with basket weaving and music appreciation. You are going to take a full load of difficult classes throughout the years. The selection board will be able to see that you can handle the program based on your transcripts, so show them you can handle a difficult load. This next subject is up for debate, but I think this concept is correct. The selection board is looking for a person who can make it through the program, rather than someone who knows someone in the senate. Who you know may work in many places in the professional world, but it is more of the exception in this profession. I do not mean to say it does not help. Nor am I trying to say that it does not happen. But it is difficult for me to believe that an entire selection board could be influenced by one or two people, based on nothing more than someone's grandfather knowing the governor's aunt, who owes him a favor. Attempting to influence the selection board in this manner can prove to be fatal. You could ruffle feathers and bias the board member's opinions, making it very difficult for them to decide. If you can't make it through the program, why would anyone care who you know? They want dedicated people. It makes their jobs easier, and they need people who are going to make it through the courses. The college loses money if you do not make it through the program.

Their philosophy is choosing people who have proven they can handle a heavy, difficult course load and maintain a good GPA (3.0 to 4.0). It is not a written or golden rule, and the GPA rumors fly. But in my experience, a 3.0 is a good minimum. Anything below this will make it difficult to be competitive.

Volunteer work is also a good thing to have along with your observation hours. I put in more than the recommended time, but I did it for myself. I really wanted to make sure I wanted to be in the profession before I leaped into the program. Observation hours are required in most, if not all, programs across the nation, and they are there to force people to get a good look at the profession. I think it is a great idea, and it also proves how serious the profession is about getting people into the program who are prepared and motivated to be a part of the science of physical therapy. Make sure you get into all the different settings. It is important that you do so, because physical therapy is very different in many ways. Acute care is very different from outpatient care, like pediatric care is different from the professional sports setting.

I work in a hospital that is very close to a small four-year college, and many students come through, trying to get their observation hours. Most of them work a year or so as a tech, and this is a good way to get your time in and your feet wet. I am not able to influence the selection board, so that is not why these future PT students come to work. The board does look at your work experience, so being a PT tech for a year or two while you get your prerequisite classes completed shows that you have worked in the setting. And if you think about it, anyone would be able to see your dedication and motivation in a sincere light. If you work as a PT tech for a couple of months or a couple of years, you will have a good understanding of this profession. You will be able to determine if it is right for you, and the selection board must feel the same way. Some of my techs come back from the interview and say that working as a tech helped them answer some of the questions. They were more prepared because they had a chance to experience some of the healthcare issues related to PT. They had seen them firsthand. I am not claiming that being a PT tech will ensure your placement in the PT program. I have seen PT techs turned down or placed on the alternate list, so it is not something that must be done. I never worked as a tech, and as I stated before, I got in on the first try. I do think it is a good way for students to experience the world of physical therapy before going into the field.

Once you have completed your prerequisites and have applied for the program, sit back and enjoy as much free time as you can, because if you get accepted, you are in for a long, hard ride. If you get a letter requesting an interview, you are on your way but the battle is not over. Preparing for the interview is a difficult task, but you will have been through so much by this time that you should have what it takes to remain calm and do a good job. My suggestions for this process are very simple, and I do not claim that they are the only way. But this is what I experienced. I sat in with three other applicants. The panel of interviewers was made up of three professors, and they explained the process, made us feel comfortable, and began the interview. This is not the only way interviews are performed and you may experience something totally different. But I think it would be safe to say that most interviews follow along these lines. The board members asked questions and allowed us to answer. They did not direct the questions to us individually. Anyone could go first, but everyone had to give an answer to the question. If you are certain that you are knowledgeable and capable of answering a question, then go first. If you are not, however, do not try to make something up just to be first. I never answered first or second. I always let everyone else answer the question before I gave my answer. It gave me time to think, and it also gave me the insight to provide a more in-depth answer. After hearing what everyone else had to say, I was able to draw from his or her good and bad points. The only way this can backfire is if one of the other applicants says exactly what you are thinking. If this happens, you can always elaborate a bit more on the answer given, but keep your comments along the same lines as your original thought. Do not make up something different to be original. There is nothing wrong with having the same answer as another applicant. The truth will always set you free. Do not try and be something you are not. Do not try to impress the board with your intelligence. Just be yourself. If that is not good enough, then you were not right for them and they were not right for you. If you have any interview experience, you should know to keep your answers simple and always stick to your original thought. Do not get caught up in trying to impress. The board will see right through that. Being nervous tends to make people ramble. They seem less self-confident and appear to be reaching for the answers, like people do when they are not telling the truth. These people do not do well in the interview process, because the interviewer lacks the ability to trust them. Trust and honesty are very important. At all costs, just be yourself and you will do fine.

One last point: You may apply to several different colleges at the same time. It will increase your odds. I think the hardest thing about doing this is the out-of-state tuition. Other than that, it is not a bad idea. If you are prepared to spend the money (or I should say get the student loans), be sure this is the right profession for you. Then go for it. I should add that, if you really are not sure about this profession, take some time and think about it before you put in the hours and the money. You really do not want to wake up one day in a field you hate, with student loans that you can't afford to pay. Then you will have to quit and begin working in a new field that you are passionate about. Also watch how much you borrow, because you may also find yourself looking for the wrong job once you have your license. You may find yourself looking for the money instead of the right area of physical therapy to practice. Some settings pay more than others, and with a heavy student loan to pay back, you may be influenced to do something you do not like. Let's say you find out during one of your clinicals that the school system is the place for you but the pay is nowhere near that of a friend working in the home health setting. You may be motivated by money, which can override your passion if you are not careful.

SUMMARY

- Get all the prerequisite class information from the physical therapy program department.
- Meet with a counselor at the college you are attending and evaluate the prerequisite information you received from the PT program.
- Group harder classes together with only one or two easy ones to prove you can handle a heavy course load.
- Sign up for classes taught by professors who are going to challenge you.
- Do not use any political influence to help you get into the program.
- Maintain a minimum 3.0 GPA; score especially high in the math and science courses.
- Do volunteer work or work as a PT tech if possible.
- Be truthful in the interview and answer last if possible.
- Do not reach too deeply into the student loan till.
- If you are able, apply to several different schools.

ADDITIONAL INFORMATION THAT MAY BE REQUIRED BY THE PHYSICAL THERAPY PROGRAM

- Letters of recommendation from undergraduate instructors, physical therapists, and former employers
- An interview and an autobiography
- Knowledge of the discipline and the issues facing the profession
- One hundred hours of clinical experience in a physical therapy setting
- GRE

EXAMPLES OF PRE-REQUISITE COURSES

- Biology
- Anatomy & Physiology
- Zoology
- Exercise Physiology
- Statistics
- Chemistry
- Physics
- Psychology
- Biomechanics
- Health & Nutrition
- Advanced/Technical Writing
- Communications
- English

THE PHYSICAL THERAPY
PROGRAM

"Once you're in the program, hang on. It's a long hard ride."

Note: *I went through the program married with children, and that is not an easy task, so I may make it sound harder than what you might experience if you are single.*

I can remember the first day of class. I thought I had died and gone to heaven. I made it, and I lived off that for a while. It helped but I will never forget constantly thinking, "What if I fail a class? What if I don't make it?" And that is what drove me to study and devote all of my time to the program. I studied every night until one or two in the morning, and that included most weekends and holidays. I tried to make sure that every test I took would ensure my grade could take a serious hit if I bombed a test. This system worked and I think I carried a 4.0 for the first semester. My wife began to complain about the constant devotion to study groups, and I systematically brought it down to a 3.5 by shaving off a few hours a day to spend more time with my family. This is how it worked for me. When we completed gross anatomy, I could have passed the course with a zero on the final. It took the heat off, and that is what I lived on for two years. Trying to manage a social life during physical therapy school is possible, especially if you are very intelligent. But if you are not one of the truly gifted people with a photographic memory, spend as much time as you can on the books and pay attention in class. It is important to balance your life while in PT school. My philosophy revolved around mind, body, and spirit, and if you can balance your time to include all three, you can make it. It will be hard to discipline yourself, and most people like myself spend more time on the mind and devote the rest of the time to caffeine products to keep the mind going, instead of exercise and spiritualism. I know I did some damage to myself going through PT school. I must have gone through a six-pack or more of Diet Coke a day.

My first reservation regarding PT school was the cadaver lab. Dissecting animals in zoology is one thing, but putting a scalpel to a human is something entirely different. I was nervous, but I made it without a problem. It was my favorite class. Once you get used to the smell of the formaldehyde, every day is an adventure. We worked in four-man teams, which helped like a group therapy session does. We were all able to bounce our concerns off of one another, and we joked around to ease the tension of the task. We did not joke in a manner that was disrespectful of the humanity of the cadaver; we did everything in good taste. Each day we followed the lab manual's instructions. It directed every step of the way. And if that did not work, one of the professors would help. Dissecting and identifying structures is the game, and I loved every minute of it. We had to find all the muscles in the body, most of the circulatory and nervous system, all of the bones and bony prominences, and some of the organs. The face was the most difficult part to dissect, and if the cadaver was large or had a lot of adipose tissue or fat, it made it even harder. I can remember one day I started in on the thigh, looking for the femoral artery. Just as I got it exposed as the perfect specimen, I nicked it with my scalpel, opening a small hole. About three seconds later, one of my partners decided to attempt CPR to see what it would feel like to give a real chest compression, which in turn shot formaldehyde and old blood all over me. I can remember stopping at a local store to buy some gas right after lab. People were looking at me somewhat strangely, but I did not think much about it. I handed the cashier my money, and she distanced herself from my hand. As she handed over my change, she dropped it into my hand. When I got home I saw myself in the mirror, I knew why. I looked like I had been involved in a surgical procedure that went bad.

Once we had a good portion of the dissection procedure down, we started having test on what we had unearthed. The professors would go around and tag structures on the cadavers so we could be tested on them. This test was the hardest to prepare for. You could tell by the tension in the waiting room. While we waited to be called into the lab, one of the students got sick from being so nervous. He threw up in a trash can. We proceeded like nothing had happened, because if we concentrated on why he threw up it would affect our performance. The rest of the courses were just like any college course: bookwork and a lot of it. For the most part pathophysiology, kenisiotherpy, cardiology, growth and development, and statistics, were among the hardest courses. I think it all depends on the professor. Some of it is the material, but most of my fellow students would agree these five areas are the hardest of all the program courses. Practicals with modalities and treatment techniques would be next most difficult, and clinical rotations weighs in as the least difficult. Trying to stay awake during lecture after staying up till one or two studying the night before for a difficult test was easier said than done. And that is were the Diet Coke came into play. My advice to any student is to align yourself with a good study group. Make sure you find a group that is serious about learning, because if you get mixed into the party crowd, you could be in for a surprise during midterms and finals. Remember this too: You are going to be using what you learn every day for the rest of your professional career. Everything in the physical therapy program is there for a reason, and it will serve you well to know it. It is not just memorization either. Understanding is essential for your success in the real world. I know I have not spent that much time on the actual curriculum, but PT school (aside from cadaver lab and the practical, hands-on experience) is like any college course you have ever taken. Just know that you will be in the books most of the time. If you study hard during your prerequisite courses, especially science and math, you will have less trouble in PT school. Actually learning the material, instead of memorizing and dumping it after the test, is the way to ensure that you will have less trouble with PT school.

PRACTICALS AND CLINICAL ROTATIONS

PRACTICALS

Physical therapists use specialized techniques to perform treatments. You will first attend a lecture in the typical classroom setting or lecture hall. These classes are specifically designed to provide you with information regarding practical application. The classes involve anatomy, physiology, pathophysiology, and etiology; they tie the bookwork to the hands-on application. You will then attend the practical class. That involves the hands-on application. The instructors will demonstrate and explain the principles behind the application of the technique or treatment. You will be asked to pick a partner, one of your classmates, and you will practice the procedure. The instructor will observe your technique and assist you with any corrections if needed. Once this process is completed, you will be asked to perform or demonstrate the procedure in front of the instructor and he or she will grade your accuracy. Let's look at an example outside the medical arena to make it easy. If you have ever worked anywhere, you had to learn some of the procedures, like working the cash register in a department store. Someone had to teach you how to use the machine, and that person probably made sure you could demonstrate your competency. The PT practicals are no different except for one thing. Instead of just being taught how the cash register is operated, you must learn to dismantle the register, memorize the name of every working part, and know its function and how the system's parts work together to perform cash register functions. You must also be able to determine system malfunctions according to system errors and repair them.

- Gross Anatomy: Dismantle the Register
- Physiology: Systems, Parts, Function, and Relation To Operation
- Pathophysiology: System Malfunctions
- Practicals: Repair and Maintenance

CLINICAL ROTATIONS

Once you get some of the course work and the practicals out of the way, you will be given a list of clinical affiliation sites to choose from. This list is comprised of physical therapy settings that choose to accept students for training purposes. Most hospitals and outpatient settings take on students without hesitation. They use the students as free labor—just kidding. The primary goal is to provide a learning experience for the students. In most cases, the students shadow a therapist for a few days before being allowed to treat patients. It all depends on the experience level of the student. Once you have attended several rotations, most clinical instructors turn you loose quickly, and supervision is at a distance instead of within arm's reach. Clinical rotations are designed to let you get your feet wet by practicing your new skills with actual patients. You will be able to experience the real world of PT. You will go out into the hospitals and outpatient clinics under the supervision of a licensed physical therapist, and you will be able to perform the skills you learned in the practical classes. You will be provided with a booklet of information prepared by the PT program instructors that you will give to your clinical instructor at the hospital or outpatient setting. This booklet contains information on the practical applications you have been taught; it lets the clinical instructor know what areas of practice you should be capable of performing. The clinical instructor assigns the appropriate task to be performed and grades you on your competency. So let's go back to the cash register example. You are now able to work the register with a customer standing in front of you. If anything should go wrong with the register, you should be able to take the information you have learned from lecture and the practicals and repair the problem while your boss watches and the customer waits. Let me state this now: I think everyone has the potential to learn, but only the people who truly love auto mechanics would sit in lecture for a couple of years to learn everything they could about cars. I could not sit in class all day, tear a car apart, and learn what each part does in relation to the other parts to make the automobile work. And this is not because mechanics don't make much money. They do. I just don't care about cars that much. I like the physical body: the muscle, skeletal, nervous system. I like knowing how it works, so PT is interesting to me and that is the key, not how much money I can make doing it. Ask yourself this question; if mechanics were professionally accepted on the same level as physicians and the pay was almost equivalent, would you go into automobile repair? Make sure you are willing to take the human body apart, sit in lectures for hours, and learn how all the parts work together to make the body run, because you have to be very interested to make it through. Money will motivate many, but only the truly dedicated students will really succeed. By the way, if you are interested in auto mechanics, I know a few mechanics who make more money than some physicians, and they are not on call twenty-four hours a day. Nor do they have to worry about carrying malpractice insurance. Do not get me wrong. People who have no interest other than making money make it through the PT program. I am sure you have come in contact with a few people in a professional career that you could see right through. You knew they did not like the profession they chose. You could see the anguish in their faces. You could tell they were disgusted with the career choice by the way they treated you as a customer. Make sure you do not wind up just like them; that is all I am trying to convey.

SETTINGS

The examples you are about to read could be encountered in each setting, however, you may never deal with any of these issues throughout your entire career. I am only expressing the truth about what you could encounter in order to prepare you to choose the setting in which you will begin to practice. If you never experience anything remotely similar to what you read in this book, it means you chose the right setting in which to practice according to your specific professional goals. You also chose an environment filled with medical professionals who truly care about patients, and I hope in some way this book will have helped you make that decision.

AREAS OF PRACTICE

Acute Care
Administration
Aquatics

Cardiopulmonary Rehabilitation

Clinical Electrophysiology

Education

Geriatrics

Hand Rehabilitation

Home Health

Hospice

Industry Ergonomics and Safety Education

Military Service

Neurology

Oncology

Orthopedics

Pediatrics

Private Practice

Research

School System

Sports

Veterans' Affairs

Women's Health

SPECIALIZATION/CREDENTIALS

The following specialty areas are recognized according to the American Physical Therapy Association.

CCS: Cardiovascular and Pulmonary Certified Specialist

ECS: Clinical Electrophysiologic Certified Specialist

GCS: Geriatric Certified Specialist

NCS: Neurologic Certified Specialist

OCS: Orthopedic Certified Specialist

PCS: Pediatric Certified Specialist

SCS: Sports Certified Specialist

NURSING HOME

POSITIVE

The nursing home setting is one of the most rewarding areas in healthcare today. Working with the senior citizen population is by far the best patient care setting I have ever experienced in PT. Senior citizens are grateful for everything we do to help them regain independence. They have a different set of values. They experienced hard times such as war and somehow learned to appreciate life and people a bit more than other generations. Any setting that allows you to see your work pay off renders a feeling of accomplishment, and sometimes that is all it takes to keep you coming back for more. The home you are housed in will also make a difference. Some of the homes will not be as nice as others, and in most cases they will have a distinct odor. However, I have been privileged to work in some that reminded me of five-star hotels with nursing stations. These homes are rare, but they can be a joy to work in. In the nursing home setting, you will be challenged by cognitive disorders such as Alzheimer's dementia, organic brain syndrome, cerebral vascular accident or stroke, and many others. These diagnoses will be tough to deal with, and your skills will be enhanced by the sheer fact that you will learn how to use improvisation. You will take what you have been taught about the body and apply it without the full cognitive effort of your patient. You will find yourself working on mobility at one of the lowest levels. The concentration in this setting is keeping the patient mobile: transferring, performing bed mobility activities, ambulating, and performing pressure-relief measures. You will screen patients and provide training for restorative aids or certified nursing staff members to perform restorative programs like ambulation training (walking), range of motion (ROM), activities of daily living (ADL), and many more mobility oriented activities. You may become involved with wheelchair evaluations, however, occupational therapy seems to have this market cornered in some areas. You may be expected to perform environmental assessments for the nursing home staff members, and if you are good, you will request to be a part of this process and the safety committee. It will be challenging every day, and you can feel like you are making a difference in people's lives in this setting. I recommend the nursing home setting based on the patient care and the overall personal satisfaction and gratification, however, the negatives can outweigh the positives. If the home is not set up in the right manner, the success of the home can be limited. The quality of therapy provided depends on the management philosophy of the rehabilitation management company and the nursing home owner, and administration team.

NEGATIVE (REMEMBER THIS IS NOT THE CASE IN ALL NURSING HOME SETTINGS.)

The nursing homes in the U.S. are not trying to lose money. They are like any other business, and making money is part of the business. Trying to provide a service for the patients is too, and many homes are providing quality care on a daily basis. But oftentimes the powers that be get lost in the game of patient care versus making money and tend to lean toward the side of making money. The political structure, or the hierarchy, takes the person watching the money away from the actual daily grind of what is going on with the patient care, and that can lead to major problems. The administrators are worried about keeping the nursing staff, physicians, patients, and family members happy, and at the same time, they have to manage the bottom line. Oftentimes they can find themselves in meetings, giving in to the money side of the struggle, and when this happens the patient care can suffer.

Before jumping into this setting, make sure the nursing home has a restorative program. It is very important. You and the patients will depend on it more than anyone else in this setting regarding the continuation of mobility once the patients are discharged from therapy services. If the home does not have an active restorative program, you will have trouble discharging patients. You will find that the patient you worked with a month ago is having problems because no one continued the mobility or ADL activities you and the patient worked so hard to attain. Patients will soon find their way back to your caseload. And guess what. The nursing home and rehab company will make money because you will pick them back up and start billing Medicare again. This is a vicious cycle that appears to be sliding by the intermediaries or Medicare.

Medicare has a system of checks and balances in place today that helps ensure that fraud and abuse is kept at a low level, but these things still exist. The PPS, or perspective payment system, helps maintain rehabilitation integrity by providing a picture of the patient and the care delivered daily. Many management companies try to maximize the rehabilitation revenue by manipulating the RUG, or resource utilization group. They treat the RUG level instead of the patient. The RUG is dependent on the amount of minutes and treatment diagnoses used, and more treatment minutes equals higher revenue codes, which allows the rehab company and or the nursing home to render more money. The system is set up to deliver more care to the patient, but in many cases the RUG is manipulated because the therapists are overwhelmed by the caseload and paperwork. They also find it hard to spend a preset amount of time with each patient because the treatment time is dependent on many different factors. The factors that limit treatment time are the patient eating, bathing, having a bowel movement, going to a doctor's appointment, being medically unstable, playing bingo, and the list really goes on forever. Trying to juggle all of these things and come up with a preset number of minutes is very difficult. If therapists are not careful, they will find themselves manipulating or falsifying documents to satisfy the rehab company and maintain their jobs. Pressure from student loans, marriage, and mortgages can make therapists fall into a trap that could cost them everything, including their licenses. For more information on Medicare rules and regulations, I recommend the Centers for Medicare and Medicaid Services Web site. You will find a wealth of information regarding rehabilitation practice guidelines on this site, and I recommend you look at it before you begin to practice. If you find yourself having trouble, just keep hunting and pecking. You will become more familiar with the site by trial and error. Another great place to begin your search for this type of information will be the American Physical Therapy Association Web site. This site has sections on everything you will ever have questions about, and I recommend you familiarize yourself with it before you begin practicing.

I know this information sounds negative, but if I do not tell you the truth, then who will. I am trying to show you the difficulties in all the different settings to help you decide what to look for and what questions to ask during job interviews. The best advice must provide you with the truth about all of the different aspects.

In most nursing home settings, a contract company manages the rehab portion, and this can put a barrier between the nursing home administrator and the staff therapists right off the bat. The therapists are not actual employees of the nursing home, and the nursing home administrator can persuade the rehab management company to a degree, based on the management company's motivation to maintain the contract. The rehab management company is motivated to keep the administrator happy, so some lean toward maintaining the contract rather than maintaining ethical principles. For an example, if a physical therapist wants to discharge a patient for failure to participate or failure to progress and the patient, family, or physician is not happy about the decision, the administrator is going to hear about it. The rehab manager will get a call from the administrator; the manager might feel the contract is in jeopardy because of the situation and may attempt to motivate the therapist to reconsider the decision. Medicare rules and regulations and the state licensure laws pressure the therapist to stick to the decision. The therapist is now faced with a job-threatening ethical choice. If the therapist stands up for what is truly an objective-based professional opinion and discharges the patient, he or she could be fired. Well, maybe not fired, but the pressure to keep the patient and the nursing home administrator happy will be expressed, and the therapist in this situation will think twice the next time he or she tries to discharge a patient. It is just human nature. The unseen pressure will drive a person to go against objectivity, and once the unspoken rule is in place, the therapist will have to make a choice whether to lie down for the sake of politics or stand up. This therapist, when walking the halls of the nursing home, will feel that everyone is thinking he or she does not like working with patients who can't progress. The family and the staff members of the nursing home will say the therapist did not give the patient a chance. Passing by these people, the therapist will feel as if he or she has done something wrong. This happens to all healthcare professionals, and physicians have to go through the same thing when they tell a family or patient there is nothing else to do for the condition. They feel the pressure of losing a customer and wonder if the patient will tell others, which may affect their practices on a public relations level. So physicians know how it feels, however, they do not rely on PT for a referral source and in most cases do not realize how that power influences the rest of the healthcare community. On the other hand, if the therapist keeps the patient on the caseload and fails to show progression, Medicare can and will deny the claim. Medicare can also claim that the therapist is committing fraud or abusing the system, which can lead to serious ramifications. If someone who knows the state PT licensure laws witnesses the event, that person can turn the therapist in to the state PT licensure board and the therapist can be investigated, which could result in suspension or the loss of the therapist's license. It is very important to be aware of these things before you jump into the nursing home setting. If I were interviewing for a job today, I would put the aforementioned into a question as a potential scenario. Depending on the response, I could decide if I wanted to work for the company right then and there. Most companies will throw this line at you: "Well, we are not in this to lose money. Are you?" Another good line is "We have to balance the therapy we provide with the bottom line." Both statements are true, but I would ask, How do you balance the bottom line? If it means putting my license in jeopardy or committing fraud, then I am not interested. If it means making the nursing home administrator happy by any means necessary, then I pass. In my opinion, it centers around the lack of respect for the PT rules and regulations and the lack of knowledge regarding the Medicare rules and regulations. But ignorance of the law is no excuse.

Note: *This is a memo to a rehab management team. Included in the memo are the problems and the resolutions that I felt would solve the issues. From this you should see a clear picture of the political struggles encountered in this environment. I worked in this setting for about a month before writing this memo and found myself demoted from director to staff therapist one week later. I quit working for the company a few months later.*

OBJECTIVE

- Determine the goals.
- Determine the problems that limit the achievement of the goals.
- Determine the resolution.
- Implement the resolution.

Goals:
Quality care
Customer satisfaction (nursing home and patient)
Staff retention and development
Promotion of public opinion
Financial gain

Problem:
Faulty management

Resolution:
Change management philosophy

HOW TO MANAGE THERAPIST

Most health care professionals enjoy helping others, but rehabilitation therapists such as physical, occupational, and speech therapists do it because they have a *need* to help and please others. They are usually perfectionists driven by an type A personality, and they have a great deal of pride in their work. The thought of failure is not an option. They constantly seek the positive feedback of the patient (physical progression and verbal praise) as a reward. Achieving the patient's physical goals and being told "I do not know how I could have gotten this far with out you" is all that is needed to push them toward another fruitful, productive day. I think that it is imperative that rehab directors and rehab companies know what drives therapists and what does not, in order to help therapists achieve their goals. This will benefit the company in terms of revenue and a quality product. I am not trying to use psychology in an attempt to swindle or misguide. I am only suggesting that, to bring about a positive outcome for all involved, we must know therapists' needs. Once we target these needs and provide the proper environment, therapists will be productive. The manager, as a therapist, should be able to harness this information from within and use it most effectively; however, when put under enough stress, he or she will lose sight of what it takes to manage himself, herself or the other therapists effectively. I am only trying to make the point that we can get lost in the hustle and bustle and quickly lose sight of how we make revenue. We want to make a name for this company that is synonymous with quality.

HOW NOT TO MANAGE A THERAPIST

Most managerial conversations are about missed minutes or RUG levels. As a therapist, my thoughts on missed minutes are as follows. If I missed minutes, it is not because I just missed them. It was because the patient was sick or my time in the facility was verging on the point of no return. I might have had to decide whether to stay and be non-productive while someone eats (and work overtime to treat the patient) or leave. So questioning me about missing minutes and asking me to make them up is like hitting me twice. I did not miss the minutes to spite the company. The patient was either sick, dying, eating, or there was something out of my control. As a manager, RUG levels are missed mainly because of lack of time to devote to RUG PPS audit logs. Most managers are therapists, so the management style required to bring about a positive result in them remains the same.

Failure is a no-no for a type A personality and not being provided with the time to manage, which results in the following statements, is not a good environment for a therapist. Missing minutes (failure), not able to treat as they see fit (failure), a manager providing negative comments (failure), improper or incorrect documentation (failure), patients and nursing home complaints (failure). "Failing to please the manager…patient care is suffering…documentation is a mess…not productive enough." Give me a paper and turn it to the want ads. Therapists will soon look for employment elsewhere and the rehab company will get the blame, thus making it harder to recruit new staff.

The goal is to make sure we do not leave the milk cow out in the rain. If she gets sick, we get less milk. If she dies, we get no milk. We do not have to feed her grain imported from France—just make sure the grain she gets is what she likes.

CHANGING THE PHILOSOPHY

If we see that we are having problems and they are consistent, then we should analyze them. I have only been with this company and in nursing home rehabilitation for a short time, but I soon realized that non-productive could become productive if I looked hard enough. No therapist wants to be a burden to a company. We like to please, so I would not look only at the therapists alone to find the problem. I would try to find out everything that hampers productivity. Do not get me wrong. Some therapists have become disgruntled and have settled for that, but most therapists are not satisfied with just letting something beat them to the point of submission.

These are things that are considered non-productive but must be accomplished to provide revenue: screens; evaluations; orders; documentation; departmental and interdepartmental meetings; PPS audit logs, time sheets; patient and family concerns; administrative and interdepartmental relations; rehab and quality assurance meetings; department and staff development; equipment ordering and tracking; wheelchair evaluations, tracking, follow up and maintenance; and staff training.

EVALUATION

The therapist is set up to fail right off the bat because the chart audit is a chore in and of itself. If the 90-L (patient admission form) is not filled out correctly, the therapist will begin searching for the data, which builds the non-productive stress level to the max. This stress makes it very difficult to concentrate on the task and thus it takes longer. If the information is not found, the therapist has to ask a nursing staff member or the Medicare coordinator. This pulls the therapist away from his or her duties and this takes time. The therapist has to stop what her or she is doing, make idle chit-chat, and then ask for help from another staff member and on and on. If a manager targets these areas and addresses them with the people responsible for providing this information, the following information will only take a few minutes to find: onset date, prior hospitalization, history, and prior level of function. The discharge plan, which falls in the social worker's corner, is a thirty-minute meeting alone because it has to be coordinated with the patient, family, and the doctor. If the therapist can't find this information, an inexperienced therapist gets the discharge plan from the patient. Well, most patients will say they want to go home and the therapist plans for that, not knowing that the family and doctor have no intention of that. If the information is not found in the chart. Coordinating with the social worker is the next step, which is another non-productive task. If it is not handled correctly, the therapist and the rehab director will be sitting in the administrator's office with a family member who wants to know who said mother could go home. This leads to more lost time.

If the nursing home makes money because the patients seen by therapists provide a reason for the patient to be skilled for Medicare part A, then the nursing home should be informed of the time constraints of the therapy department during a chart review and provide the information. If the rehab management company cannot see this, they should expect less productivity. If this rehab company would take a quick look at all the missing data it sends back to the therapy department, it would see a pattern. Analyze it, and don't just sit back and keep letting this valuable information slip past. Ask the question why, and you can find the solution.

MISSING MINUTES/RUG LEVELS

In some cases missed minutes are purely due to a lack of planning by the therapist. In some cases, it is because they do not care. In my opinion, missing minutes are caused by the lack of time given to the therapist to plan. Therapists are perfectionists, and meeting a goal they set would be a perfect way to prove their worth. They would not intentionally miss a goal.

In the case of volume overload, a therapist only does what comes naturally. As the day progresses, he or she shortens treatment sessions one by one in order to handle an increase in volume or adjust to a variety of issues. This is the reason for missed RUG levels. The manager blames the therapist for missing the minutes and later asks the therapist to make them up. If a patient has a plan of thirty minutes and the therapist misses fifteen minutes one day due to volume overload, what makes the manager think that adding fifteen or twenty to another day is appropriate. Plus the therapist missed them because he or she could not handle the volume. So is adding minutes to another day really a valid request. My guess is that you know that the duration of a treatment session assigned by the therapist is arbitrary in the first place, and you should know that because no objective measure is currently being utilized to determine the treatment time.

The truth is that the missed minutes are the manager's fault for not managing the caseload.

Example: *If a therapist has fifteen people on caseload of thirty minutes per patient, that's seven and a half hours of treatment. It is impossible to document correctly and treat effectively unless you group or dovetail constantly (while documenting), which patients and therapist alike hate. We should be looking at the planned minutes for the fifteen patients and compare that to a six- or six-and-a-half-hour day (75 percent productive). If we do not, we are setting the therapists up for failure/missed minutes.*

The milk cow cannot produce milk if she is pulling a plow.

The only way these so-called non-productive tasks can become productive is to let a lesser paid employee (non-professional) perform the job. The manager attends the meetings, manages the caseloads, treats patients as needed, and performs all other related tasks that would require professional knowledge. This enables the staff therapist to produce. If the manager is able to provide the support so the therapist can produce, the manager is in fact productive.

This is not a new idea. It has been manageable in the past in other homes with fewer demographic issues and smaller caseloads. XYZ Nursing Home is a different animal altogether so it must be handled according to need, not company protocol. The lack of management causes fallout that has to be policed eventually. Flying by the seat of your pants results in a crash eventually.

HOW TO INCREASE THE REVENUE

Don't leave the milk on the table.

We should analyze how the minutes are determined in the first place. Remember I stated earlier that the way a therapist determines the minutes is arbitrary. Well, if you look deeper, you will see that the therapist is persuaded inadvertently by his or her caseload. The measure by which he or she chooses the minutes the patient can tolerate is directly related to the number of patients on his or her caseload. This brings me to the next area of concern that I find to be a significant problem. The current philosophy is "we are not paid for the evaluation so, do it quickly."

The evaluation is the key to revenue and meeting the patients' needs. The quick fifteen-minute evaluation has lost this company money hand over fist. If the correct amount of time is taken to perform an evaluation, the therapist can determine all the areas that need attention and increase treatment minutes if necessary. A speedy evaluation that looks for the outstanding issues is limited; we should give some time to the evaluation so we can find all the areas that need attention. The manager needs to realize that a therapist is going to evaluate new patients and determine the minutes a person is capable of by first thinking about his or her current caseload. If a therapist knows that her or she has fifteen people on caseload, that therapist will not try to reach ultra high levels. The therapist knows how much time he or she has in a day to treat and adjusts accordingly. The therapist has unintentionally lost sight of the patients needs based on the caseload demand. If the manager took the time to manage, we could increase the number of minutes per patient, therapists, and revenue. If the therapist is not restricted or persuaded by the sheer volume of patients he or she will encounter, he or she will determine the minutes according to the patients' needs, thus providing more minutes of therapy to the customer. The outcome will be a satisfied patient who provides positive feedback for the therapist, which equals a happy therapist, which increases revenue. (The rehab company and nursing home are happy.)

Increase the ability for the therapist to perform and increase the revenue. That is the plan. I have more to offer, however, I have less time to complete it because of the sheer volume we are experiencing at XYZ Nursing Home.

Monie Phillips PT

ACUTE CARE HOSPITAL

POSITIVE

Acute care has become my safe haven, however, you should know that I have complete control over how I manage the department, so I am biased. However, the treatment in this setting remains one of my favorites. You will not get the satisfaction of seeing a patient through a complete rehabilitation program in most cases, but you will see small improvements daily. Most inpatient stays average four days, and that is not long. So you can see why you will not see the full rehab potential of your patients. The orthopedic floor is the most rewarding in my opinion. However, I feel this way because I am mechanically inclined. Orthopedics appeals to me the most because I can imagine the hardware (total knee replacement, total hip replacement) and what it will take to rehabilitate the patient.

The acute care setting is the best for new graduates because it sharpens the skills in regard to contraindications to treatment, which will help in any future settings. Taking vitals will prove to be a daily task, and it is very important to be able to interpret the results. Auditing the chart will also prove to be very educational; finding, interpreting, and utilizing medical information in the patient's chart is vital to quality care. It also allows new therapists to experience the healthcare process from the beginning. If therapists can see how the process works from the beginning it will give them an appreciation or provide them with a well-rounded knowledge if they venture into the home healthcare or outpatient setting at a later date. They will know what took place day one post-surgical intervention or CVA, and this information will provide them with the confidence and increased ability to treat in a rehab or outpatient setting.

Wound care is another area in the acute care setting that I love. Most therapists will agree that acute care is where you will get most of your wound care experience. Acute post-surgical wounds, chronic wounds, pressure ulcers and many other exciting skin integrity issues await you in the acute care world. If you are interested in wounds, then this is the place to be, but make sure the therapy department is active in the hospital you choose. Many hospitals use the nursing staff to perform most, if not all, of the wound care treatments.

Overall, the acute care setting is the best place to gain experience in all aspects of physical therapy practices. And in most cases it allows the therapist to meet and interact with physicians, which can help establish a therapist's abilities. Gaining the physician's trust is essential for future relationships, and the acute care setting can be a springboard for future job opportunities. If you establish yourself in the acute care setting, you can move into an outpatient clinic and physicians may refer to the clinic, which is a plus in marketing yourself. It has been my experience that the acute care therapist spends a great deal of time communicating with the entire healthcare team, utilization review, the floor nurses, and the physicians. This process of daily notes, telephone conversations, and verbalization helps the new graduate learn the political world of healthcare and will provide valuable communication skills for the future.

NEGATIVE (REMEMBER THIS IS NOT THE CASE IN ALL ACUTE CARE SETTINGS.)

The acute care setting is set up under Medicare with a system called DRG, diagnosis related group. This means the hospital gets paid a lump sum depending on the admitting primary diagnosis. So the hospital gets paid one amount no matter what services are provided to the patient. This is why acute care has become my favorite place to work; it is in my opinion the purest of all settings. Medicare hit the nail on the head with this process, and it works out well for all involved in my opinion. However, because of the DRG system, the acute care group in the therapy department is no longer looked upon as a revenue maker, and this negates most of the department's bargaining power. Without the ability to make revenue, the rehab manager finds it difficult to provide for the acute department. The only way the rehab team can improve revenue is to manage the SNF unit, which is reimbursed like a nursing home, and you already know about the problems in that setting. Inpatient rehabilitation is another way to provide revenue, but Medicare is also closing the door on this setting's reimbursement rates. Remember rehab department managers are in charge of all three settings (acute care, inpatient rehab, and SNF), and they can become biased. If you are not making money, your voice is silenced in most cases. Therefore, it is possible that rehab managers are not going to hear the acute care needs unless they are good managers. If they are not fair to all or if only the revenue generating therapies motivate the manager, it can become a nightmare for the acute care team.

I have been in hospital settings where I walked into volume overload every day. I quit shortly after I tried to communicate my concerns about the lack of quality care. My concerns fell on deaf ears, and I had no choice but to look for another source of employment. Overall in the acute care setting, not having the ability to bargain for acute care needs, due to the lack of revenue making capability and the sheer volume overload, seems to be the biggest concern regarding the money side.

Problems with nursing has got to be the biggest issue overall in the acute care hospital, and it will take some time to explain. So sit back for a history lesson, because it is important to know the history of your profession. You would not get married without knowing a little history, so why jump into PT without researching the history. The nursing field conceived physical therapy, and I do not think it is ready to let us leave home just yet. During World War I, nurses began the difficult task of assisting injured soldiers in regaining functional independence, and from there it grew. More complex treatments were directed toward more specific pathological diagnoses. This specialization in nursing services soon became a separate and distinct entity, and the field of physical therapy was created. So we are the children of nursing, and we have to respect nurses for what they have done and do every day. However, over the last decade, nursing has seen a dramatic change in the number of admissions to nursing school programs, and in my experience, we have seen an entirely different group applying. I have seen bankrupt farmers going through nursing clinicals and they did a great job; however, it is hard for me to believe that they chose nursing because of a Florence Nightingale experience they saw in a movie. I question their motives, but nonetheless they are coming from all different walks of life, and I am afraid that poor working conditions and low incomes have driven the nurturing females into more rewarding professions. I refer to females and most people scream "chauvinist," but long ago the profession was predominantly female. However, that is not all I am referring to in this case. I have worked with many male nurses in my time, and they are very capable and very good at caring, so please do not get me wrong. I am only trying to express my opinion on the type of students the nursing programs are seeing today as compared to yesteryear. Nurturing and caring for patients is the primary prerequisite for the nursing field, and it takes a special person to fill the shoes of a good nurse. Therefore, when I call nursing the greatest problem you will encounter in this setting, I mean the shortage of nurses and the type of people who are now in this profession. Nursing, as an entity is not the problem. The shortage of nurses and the poor quality of new graduates is the problem in a nutshell. Poor education because of the lack of nursing teachers and the overall change in the students being admitted is the reason. And this is not only my opinion. Pick up any magazine related to healthcare and see for yourself. Nursing is in a crisis, and I am not sure this nation has ever seen anything like it. All of what I just stated can be summed up like this: The nurses that got into the field because they have a connection or need to care for people are trying to do just that, however, they are being overworked because the less attentive nurses or the ones that got into the field for the money and stability pawn as much work off on them as they can. They lazy nurse can bring an entire floor to its knees. The poor attitude oozes over onto everyone and it kills the caring spirit, which is what nursing is all about. On top of that, the shifts are crazy enough to make anyone scream for help. Overall, remember that I do not feel that nurses are the problem, however, the issues pertaining to the shortage that I have stated will affect your experience in the acute care hospital setting.

So now you have a little history, and it is time to delve of into the problems you may encounter because of what was previously mentioned. Now, I know that I started out with only one problem but really it is not that easy. There are multiple problems, but the following two problems will affect your job satisfaction the most: the nursing shortage and the fact that physical therapy overlaps, or goes hand in hand with, nursing services. Remember the PT field was conceived and nurtured by nurses until it grew up and left home. Now, how could this affect you as a new PT? Well, the services that the physical therapy department provides on a daily basis revolve around mobility. We evaluate and treat patients who primarily have limitations with mobility. Once we begin treatment, we are thinking of the overall well-being of the patient. We want to treat the physical limitations and help with the pulmonary system and the bowel and bladder functions. When we have completed the therapy session, we request that the patient sit up in a chair instead of lying down in bed all day, which compromises the pulmonary and bowel system. Lying flat of your back all day and night with only a brief period of mobilization will allow fluid to collect in the lungs, which can cause pulmonary complications. Lying in bed day and night can also cause constipation, which can also cause serious medical complications. Well, once we convince the patient to sit up in a chair, we are off to see the rest of our patients. As soon as the patient hits the call button and requests assistance to get back into bed, in most hospital settings around the nation, the nurse will call PT to perform the task. Now I need to clarify one thing, and this will sound terrible but it is the truth. Before the DRG system began, the hospital was paid according to each service provided, fee-for-service. Well, many rehab managers took advantage of this system and requested that nursing call PT to get patients back to bed so they could bill for transfer training. Getting the patient back to bed would allow the therapist to perform a training session, a service that equals payment. If the PT profession had concentrated on providing skilled services instead of grasping after every dollar, this would not be the problem that it is today. This is not entirely a fraudulent idea or practice, however, in some cases it was abused and thus the reason for the DRG system. Now physical therapists are finding it hard to break the old systems put into place under the old payment system, and nurses are still calling the therapist to put the patient back to bed. Utilizing therapists for skilled services only is essential in today's times, however, nurses are not easily convinced that they should be the ones that feel the repercussions. Every time Medicare creates a new system or restricts the reimbursement, a duty seems to fall back on the nurses and they feel as if they are the dumping ground. Many hospitals utilize the certified nursing assistants or male orderlies to perform these tasks, and I think that works in most cases. But like nurses, they seem to be understaffed and underpaid. I think that I may need to mention that physical therapy putting patients back to bed was not the sole reason for Medicare implementing the DRG system. Many other issues contributed to the decision. Human nature is the main reason, and the systems put into place today are like putting a lock on your personal items. I never really understood this phrase until just recently: *Locking up your possessions keeps an honest man honest, because thieves will break the lock if they want to steal.* Medicare is trying to keep healthcare professionals honest, and the DRG system is doing a good job.

Over the last ten years, I have come to an understanding about payment and treatment. I am very comfortable with the systems in place, because I understand what the payer is trying to accomplish. I mentioned medical necessity in the nursing home setting, and again it is a term you should get familiar with right off the bat. It is used throughout all settings and it is the key to payment. Physicians provide us with the primary diagnosis, and it is our job to compliment that with a treatment diagnosis. In the CMS guidelines, you will find a section regarding therapy services that explains this in detail. I will give you enough information to get you started and help you apply it to the acute care setting. Oftentimes a physician writes an order for the patient to be out of bed or for nursing services to ambulate the patient twice a day. This order does not read "PT evaluate and treat." Well, the physician returns and finds that the patient has not been out of bed or walked at all. The next thing that happens is an order for physical therapy is written, and the only reason for this is that nursing did not provide the service. The physician knows that PT will do an evaluation, and there will be a request for mobility. However, in most cases the patient has an improper primary medical diagnosis, one that does not support the need for physical therapy. A urinary tract infection has not been proven medically to cause skeletal abnormalities. Nor has it caused people to develop balance disturbances or muscle weakness. That just cannot happen. People can become debilitated from lying in bed for too long, but debility is a red flag diagnosis for payers. They feel that the patient should have been mobilized by the certified nursing staff or the orderlies. Think of it like this: Would you pay a lawyer to cut your grass? Well having PT treat a patient who does not have any physical, skeletal, muscular, or nerve pathology is like paying a lawyer to cut your grass. If nursing would have taken the time to get the patient up or followed the physicians order to begin with, PT would have never been consulted. If the physical therapist evaluates the patient and begins treatment, he or she is in violation of the Medicare rules and regulations and the state licensure laws so this is a very sore subject. You have to remember the nursing shortage that I mentioned is not helping the problem. Fewer nurses means less time to provide patients with the proper care; thus more services are being dropped or pushed over to physical therapy and other ancillary departments. I do not blame the nursing staff for this problem, but it is a problem and it must be dealt with now in my opinion. In most cases the nurses have no idea what PT has to deal with in regard to medical necessity. Their primary goal is not to make life difficult for therapists. They are only trying to make it through the twelve-hour shift without a family member or physician screaming too loudly at them. They are the center of the patient's care, and this is a huge responsibility. They are pulled from one station or floor to another and are expected to memorize and regurgitate information regarding each patient on the spot at any time. You may have thought that I had a cold heart toward nurses, but remember they are our mothers. And I might add that my wife is an RN. I really would like to write another book about the problems that nurses face on a daily basis, but I do not feel I am qualified. I do know what I have witnessed, and I am here to say you could not pay me to be a nurse.

Administration can also contribute to the problem as well. Nursing has been around much longer than physical therapy or any other allied health profession, so most nursing administrators have a large voice in the administrative circles. They have been in the system much longer. They set up shop years ago, if you know what I mean. It is very clear to me that the problem is going to intensify, and no one really knows just how bad it is going to get. I do not blame nursing for any of the things I have stated. Healthcare is changing and change is not something people like. So it is going to be a tough road ahead. Just hang on for the ride, and make sure you do not let any of these issues drive you to manipulate the system. You could find yourself standing before a Medicare review board or the state PT board. You may think this sounds extreme, but when a couple of million dollars is billed and there is no documentation to prove medical necessity or the need for skilled therapy services, watch out. I can almost guarantee no one from the hospital will be there to defend you.

Note: *This is a letter I wrote to administration regarding some issues we were having when transferring patients from the acute care setting to the skilled nursing unit.*

UTILIZATION REVIEW

Therapy services are rarely if ever consulted regarding the transfer of a patient from the acute care setting to the SNF. The majority of patients transferred to the skilled unit do not qualify for rehab hospital settings, and that in and of itself makes it difficult to qualify them for therapy on the SNF. If they are qualified for the SNF, they only require one to three weeks of skilled treatment, secondary to the poor prognosis. This is the reason they did not qualify for rehab in the first place. The hospital would benefit from promoting the SNF unit and attracting patients with good rehab potential. Instead we are sending most of our patients to our competition for services that could be rendered at our SNF unit.

QUESTIONS

Why are we referring Medicare patients to rehab hospitals when we are capable of providing this service?

If patients and physicians are requesting transfers to rehab hospitals, why are they?

What are we doing to promote the SNF unit as a rehab facility?

Candidates for acute care are qualified by the SNF nursing staff. What criteria are they going by? Is therapy considered prior to asking the physician to skill the patient through therapy services?

Which department in the hospital is responsible for knowing the current Medicare guidelines, bulletins, or changes to Medicare rules and regulations?

How are the involved staff members notified of these changes?

What system is in place to ensure each department is knowledgeable or capable of interpreting Medicare rules?

What system is in place for ensuring departments are keeping up with Medicare rules, regulations, and the constant changes?

In general, who is currently making sure all involved staff members are on the same page concerning patient care and Medicare rules and regulations?

RESTORATIVE NURSING CARE

Once patients are on the skilled nursing unit, they are allowed to stay primarily based on how long rehab services will treat them. Therapy becomes the reason the patient is on the skilled unit, the reason for billing Medicare. Once the therapy department has attempted to progress the patient and as stated above, treatment usually takes one to three weeks. The patient, family, hospital, physician, and SNF nursing staff are all relying on the rehab department to continue services until placement is determined. The appropriate out at this point is to discharge the patient to a restorative nursing program, however, the SNF unit currently has no restorative program, which makes it impossible. This issue ends with the therapy department being told to continue therapy, which is considered fraudulent in nature by Medicare standards.

PHYSICIANS

Therapy promptly informs the appropriate personnel that they can no longer provide skilled services due to a lack of progress. But the patient's family is not ready for the patient to go home and they have not decided on the placement for the patient. The physician is motivated to keep the patient based on several factors. The physician may need more time to sort out medical problems or monitor the patient for a short time. Or the physician might be motivated to keep the patient's family members happy and therefore does not discharge them. The therapy department communicates with social services and the physician regarding the intent to discharge the patient from therapy services, however, the patient remains on the SNF unit. The therapy department is told to continue treatment, which places the therapists in a position to commit Medicare fraud. This also violates state licensure rules and regulations.

BILLING

The billing department is removed from the actual care of the patient. They have no way of knowing if the patient care is reasonable and necessary. The billing department does not have any idea if the information it receives from the nursing documentation is correct. They are motivated by getting the claim processed in a timely manner and making sure the forms are accurate enough to bill. The SNF staff members are motivated by the census and the hospital by getting paid. It all revolves around keeping the patient qualified for payment, skilled services. Therapy is being used to qualify the patient. But in most cases the patient does not qualify for therapy.

MEDICARE

Medicare reviewers will kick back claims that show lack of progress or no progress of patients' physical status. If the claim is submitted and the MDS and therapy notes do not line up or do not reflect the same information, the claim will be denied. We currently have no system or procedure in place to make sure the nursing notes, the MDS, and the therapy notes are concurrent with each other. The lack of knowledge regarding rehab services and Medicare billing and coverage of services is putting the hospital at risk for Medicare audits or reviews.

RESPONSIBILITY

Each healthcare professional is ultimately responsible for providing patient care that is considered by medical standards to be reasonable and necessary. Each healthcare professional is responsible for protecting the Medicare program by knowing the rules and regulations.

DISCHARGE

To make sure the patient and family are informed of Medicare part A billing procedures and timeframes for skilled therapy services, who is providing this information to them and helping them during the discharge planning procedure? Currently rehab services notify the physician, SNF nursing staff, and social services promptly. However, the physician is responsible for the patient and they make the final decision, which is the proper procedure. But if the patient can no longer be considered skilled for therapy and the rehab staff member discharges the patient, everyone involved appears to be dissatisfied with the decision. At this point in the patient's treatment, everyone involved has foreknowledge that therapy's intention is to discharge the patient. Requesting therapy continue treating the patient for payment reasons is fraudulent. This goes back to restorative care issues, or the lack of a restorative program. The restorative program can be used for this purpose and serves as a cushion for extended needs of the physician, e.g. to continue monitoring a medical problem. It also allows the family to make placement arrangements.

Note: *This is a letter I wrote to myself at my first acute care hospital setting. I did it to figure out what we could do to solve some of the problems we faced every day.*

PROBLEMS

- Fluctuating patient load.
- Acuity Level changes between floors—even on the same floor—and changes at different phases of patients' stay.

- No time for meetings about the ever-changing policies and procedures on all the floors.
- No communication between PT and floor nursing staff.
- No communication between physicians and PT staff on any floor.
- No time for communication between PT staff members in acute.
- Lead PT unable to perform admin duties and see patients.
- Therapists do not and are unable to do D/C summaries.
- Administration does not want patients to complain but does not listen to why they complain; decreased primary care staff is the main concern.
- Hospital trying to keep employees down to just enough people to run a skeleton crew, however, the crew is not prepared to handle crunch times and is not looking at acuity level.
- Most patients complain about bath times, never being bathed, or never seeing a nurse or doctor.
- CNA or nursing staff does not perform CPM applications correctly.
- The patient calls and no one comes, or he or she does not come in a timely manner.

OUTPATIENT

POSITIVE

This setting is were the real art of physical therapy practice is performed. It is treasured by many and can be the biggest revenue source in existence for business-minded physical therapists today. I am kidding about the "real art" statement, but most physical therapists consider outpatient to be the only place real PT services are delivered. This is not true, but the more fine-tuned applications do take place in this setting. This does not mean it is any more important than any other PT setting. Each setting has its own spot in the specialty arena, and no physical therapist can say that he or she felt comfortable walking into an I.C.U. (intensive care unit) for the first time for the task of getting a patient bedside. Specialty is in the eye of the beholder, and as I stated, each area has skilled services that are just as complex as any other setting.

Outpatient services deal with pain and muscle weakness, back injuries, workers compensation, sports injuries, and many more. The rewards come on a daily basis. However, failure is also something you will face on a daily basis. In most cases, the rewards outweigh the failures, and taking pain away from a chronic back injury can last a lifetime, and that can make your year. Another success that is common in this setting is having things you were taught in school materialize in front of you. I can remember thinking "this really works" on many occasions, and as I got a few years under my belt, I began to realize the magnitude of the information I had received during my training and that every subject had meaning and purpose. Outpatient really opens your eyes to the science of physical therapy, and the personal and professional growth potential is endless. Just because you were taught the science does not mean it ends there. You will be able to start your own mental database. After time, patterns will begin to form, and treatment strategies will become second nature. Evaluations will become painless, communication will flow from the patient's mouth without all the stories about the aunt who used alcohol to treat an injury, because you no longer ask open ended questions; time is of utmost importance. If you have ever been to a doctor, you know what I am talking about regarding the time issue. Doctors keep the questions directed to a yes or no answer, and this is done for a good reason. They only need to know the information needed to treat the problem. Listening to the patient is important, but him or her venting frustrations is not what they want to hear. They are trying to get to the root of the problem, so they direct the questions to get to it as quickly as possible. They have people waiting, and the patient knows this because he or she has spent an hour in the waiting room and twenty minutes waiting in the little exam room. The same situation takes place in most fast-paced outpatient clinics around the world every day. Every once in a while, I have been seen on time and the physician did not appear to rush me, but this is not common. Do not get me wrong. Listening to the patient is the key, but getting the information you need quickly to treat or diagnose the problem is an art, and it only comes with time.

Overall, this setting is a great place to be, and I recommend it without reservation. New graduates and seasoned therapists without outpatient experience can be a positive asset. Just make sure you are surrounded by knowledgeable, ethical therapists, and most importantly make sure the staff is "question friendly" or able to take the time to give you pointers. Bouncing ideas and treatment strategies off another therapist is a great tool, and it can provide you with a little group therapy if you are troubled about your performance. You will find that you are not alone, and as you already know, medicine is a practice. Practice means you are allowed to make mistakes. No one knows everything and even the seasoned pros do not have the answer to every problem they encounter.

NEGATIVE (REMEMBER THIS IS NOT THE CASE IN ALL OUTPATIENT SETTINGS.)

Volume overload has to be the greatest threat to quality care in this setting. If you find yourself in this situation because of the limited availability of therapists or clinics in the area, then it is less stressful. But if the volume is purely due to greed, then you are headed for burnout. The issue of money is surfacing in this book like a plague, but it needs to be mentioned because it is the truth.

Dealing with the lies patients looking for a big settlement tell is another big issue that can cause burnout. I sat in my office and watched patients get out of cars and taxi cabs, just to prove my frustration was not in vain. Most patients got out of the car with smiles on their faces. They skipped over the curb like nothing was wrong, but when they opened the door to the clinic, new people took shape. Their faces became distorted as if to say they were in pain. It became hard to treat these patients, because the objective information did not line up. Lawyers were calling to ask if information could be provided that would substantiate the inability-to-work claims. They wanted to know just how bad the damage was, in order to win the case and collect the settlement. One day, pain ratings will become truly objective, and if the insurance companies and workers' compensation people are not already working on it, I know someone is. A therapist in one of the settings I worked in told a story about a patient who came in to the clinic with a cervical collar on. She asked the patient why the doctor had prescribed the collar, and the patient replied, "My lawyer gave this to me, not my doctor." After a year of this, I learned to speak and write in a lawyer's terms. Documentation is key, and if something is not correct, you may find yourself in court trying to dig yourself out of a hole you created. Writing the term *inconsistent findings* became a daily event, and it was true. Patients would report pain that did not make sense, and the objective tests proved it. Now politics and money come into play, so let's get into it. First, below is a letter that deals with autonomy. I think it will help clear things up a bit before we get into the next section.

Note: *This letter was written for a student. It addresses autonomy in the PT profession and how it could help improve patient care. The comments made in this section or any section of this book regarding physicians and lawyers do not apply to all members of these professions. There are plenty of ethical and moral physicians and lawyers out there.*

The main reason PT autonomy will be beneficial for this state and the nation is that currently the best way to get referrals in most settings is to have a physician as a medical director. You would think that most people would take a script from a physician and go to the PT clinic of their choice, but most of the time they are told which clinic to go to, like steering in the car insurance arena. This makes it hard to thrive as an outpatient clinic without a large support group of physicians referring patients. The medical director "physician" is paid to be the medical liaison for the outpatient clinic, nursing home, home health setting, etc. Thus he has motive to refer to the clinic. If Medicare and private insurance companies begin to pay for therapy services without a script or order from a physician, services can be provided for the patient without the politics. Cutting down on the red tape and political antics is a win-win situation for everyone involved. It is my opinion that patients would choose the healthcare setting they need based on the reputation of the therapists, which takes competition to its truest level. This would also drive the quality of care to new heights. Taking the politics and the money out of the equation speaks for itself in my opinion.

In all the other settings of physical therapy, the nation would see improved quality as well. The pressure of needing the physician would be resolved, and therapists would be more inclined to treat and discharge at will, without the fear of repercussions from physicians. Currently, if the PT does something to make the physician angry, for instance discharging a patient when there is no medical necessity, and the family member and patient complain, the physician re-orders therapy to make the family happy, which puts the physical therapist in an awkward position. If the therapist does not follow the physician's orders, he or she might be in need of another job. If the therapist treats the patient, he or she is going against the state practice act, rules and regulations. Treating patients who have no potential for improvement is not ethical. Doing it to maintain physician relations is not ethical, but it happens because people are scared of losing their jobs. It is like sexual harassment cases when a supervisor is making sexual remarks to an employee. But the physical therapist/physician relationship is not looked at in this light so it goes on. Fear of retribution exists for therapists everywhere.

If physical therapists were able to treat and receive payment without referrals from physicians, the overall care of the patient would improve dramatically. The ability to maintain a good client base or caseload would be based on the quality of the work or service provided and not how politically tied the owner is to a group of physicians.

Monie Phillips PT

Meeting the bottom line is based on survival and is key to the success of the business, but it can also be the biggest threat to objective, goal-based therapy. I would like to state that I am not against making money, but I know what it can do to people. And in most situations, it has a negative influence. The fact that physician referrals drive the business means the owners of the clinic must keep the physicians happy. The lawyer's must also be happy and keep referring patients to the clinic. This should mean that quality care must prevail, and most of the time it does. The greatest factor in keeping the physician happy is keeping the patient happy, and that can lead to danger. If the person involved in an accident is sent to a clinic that is known for objective examinations and goal-based treatment, then the chances of getting a good settlement diminish. If the person returns to full functioning without problems, then what harm can be claimed except for lost wages and medical bills. I have mentioned this situation before, but I will go over it again for the outpatient setting. If a therapist discharges a patient for false or inconsistent findings or failure to comply with treatments, the patient will not be happy. The patient will tell his or her physician and lawyer, and the referrals to the clinic might diminish. One phone call from the referring physician to the owner of the PT clinic about this problem will have a strong impact. The outpatient owner and physical therapist will have to decide to continue treatment and overlook the inconsistent findings in the same situation next time if they want to continue to see referrals. Now, you may be thinking at this point that you will never do anything like this, but remember what was discussed before. Student loans, new cars, and other bills add up after college is over. Most people remember the movie *The Firm* with Tom Cruise as the leading actor. In this movie, he had to make a decision. He could join in and overlook the fraudulent undertakings or get out. The firm gave him so many nice things and provided him with a great job and salary to boot. Some clinics will do things like pay off your student loans or pay enormous salaries to get you in the game, but know there could be a deadly price to pay for these benefits.

INPATIENT REHAB

POSITIVE

This setting is rewarding and can be compared to outpatient therapy because the treating therapist can see patient progression. Watching a patient go from total dependence to independence is a very rewarding experience. Patients are normally referred from the acute care setting to inpatient rehab. The referral source fluctuates but the primary source is usually orthopedic physicians. Physiatrists are normally utilized for the medical director position, and they are very knowledgeable about physical medicine. The types of diagnoses treated in this area range from orthopedic in nature to spinal cord injuries and burns. Patients suffering from cerebral vascular accidents are common and comprise a large part of the caseload. Working with a team of therapists, nurses, and physicians can provide a new graduate with a great deal of support with learning experiences. The daily challenges and the variety of diagnoses seen in this setting will also add to the great learning environment. This setting is a great place for new graduates and seasoned professionals alike. For the new graduate, it is necessary to work with a seasoned professional in this setting. You will need guidance. The rehab unit is usually well-outfitted with equipment and has plenty of room to treat effectively. Physical therapy technicians are usually found in this setting and they can prove to be very helpful, however, the ability to utilize the techs is dependent upon Medicare rules, regulations, and this may vary between individual state licensure laws. Patients' rooms are situated around the therapy gym, and in most cases the patients have scheduled treatment times. The patients are brought into the gym by the certified nursing assistants or the PT techs, which is very helpful for the treating therapist in regards to productivity.

NEGATIVE (REMEMBER THIS IS NOT THE CASE IN ALL INPATIENT REHAB SETTINGS.)

The most common complaint in this setting revolves around patient overload. Dovetailing is commonly utilized to help increase the productivity, and the weekly group therapy sessions also helps the therapist catch up on paperwork. However, these tactics decrease the quality of care in my opinion. Dovetailing involves overlapping fifteen minutes of treatment time between two patients. The patient being treated performs activities, or in most cases takes a rest break, while the next patient begins a warm-up session. Whatever you want to call it, I think it sounds like a way to make more money. The ideal picture for the manager is to see one person walking around the gym with a tech and two patients working with the therapist. One patient is usually working on a mat table doing exercises while the other is doing the same thing on the same table or one nearby. If you do not have to put your hands on the patients, ask yourself the question, How skilled is the service? Medical necessity comes to mind when a tech is exclusively treating any patient, and repetitive ambulation to increase distance is not a skilled service. Counting repetitions for a patient who is independent with the exercise routine is not therapy and should not be considered skilled. Prescribing the exercise is skilled. Assessing the patient's progress is skilled. But counting reps is not. The therapist should be providing a service that no one else can without extensive training. In some settings, you will find one or two therapists with specialized skills who treat one patient at a time. They are very hands-on oriented and also very effective. These therapists stand out in these settings, and it usually means they stood up to the managers as to how they conduct themselves ethically. They treat with the objective goal-based mindset I have been discussing, and I hope you follow their example. If we got to the root of the problem, we would find that some of the people do not qualify for inpatient rehab, but to keep the patient relationship, the physician, and the bottom line happy, someone must treat them. The question is will that therapist be you. The patients need to have someone assist them, and most of the time, they need to be motivated. But the responsibility to progress is truly up to them. Keeping them on the caseload because they will not progress unless someone forces them to comply is not ethical. The responsibility must be placed where it is truly needed without fear of repercussions. However, making money motivates and fear dominates. The result is a plague that is bankrupting our Medicare system; the lawsuit settlements are going in the pockets of the lawyers and the very people we are trying to heal. Fear that has developed over the years has taken the power away from the professionals. They no longer feel that the patient has a role or responsibility in the healthcare delivery system. The rehab makes money from the therapists putting their consciences and licenses on the line by treating patients who could be discharged if they would follow the prescribed routine. If you find yourself bored stiff counting reps, it is your soul reaching out to you. If you get a funny feeling in your stomach when you try to discharge a patient because the physician, rehab manager, and patient all disagree, it is your soul trying to tell you that something is not right. One day you will find yourself treating against your will, and the few true therapy candidates you do treat will not be able to keep your spirit up. Going to work will seem like a chore instead of a joy. Helping people will no longer be a part of your purpose. One day you will have to decide to give in and add to the problems of healthcare, quit the field, or open your own practice. If you are not careful, this corruption will creep up on you. That weird feeling in your stomach will no longer be there to warn you.

HOME HEALTH

POSITIVE

Fun can be found in home healthcare if you are the type of person who does not like to be cooped up in a gym. The money is better than that of most settings, and the autonomy is great. There is no one to worry about except the open road and the patient care. I have found this to be one of the most fulfilling experiences in physical therapy, and I recommend this setting to everyone. Like I said, you will not have to worry about any other discipline while performing your treatments, except the occasional mix up with a nurse or a certified nursing assistant, and this is not a big problem unless you are in a hurry. Working with patients in their homes is a great way to get an idea of what is really needed to help rehabilitate a person to total independence. You will actually get to work on meeting functional goals like getting in and out of a tub, getting in and out of bed, negotiating steps or stairs. The real part is working with their beds, tubs, and stairs. It is a great setting, and the patients are very grateful for your time and efforts. They like to show you pictures, and almost all of them try to feed you or send you off with fresh vegetables. They get to know you on a more personal level. Being in their homes is the icebreaker. In the home setting you can perform environmental assessments, teach safety education, and work on activities of daily living. You can do almost anything shy of modalities that require large equipment. You will encounter diagnoses that are common to rehabilitation units like CVA's, CHF, COPD, cardiac, total hip and knee replacements. These are just a few of the most common. You will become very creative and will find yourself using household objects to provide resistance during exercises and stretching activities.

NEGATIVE (REMEMBER THIS IS NOT THE CASE IN ALL HOME HEALTH SETTINGS.)

Again, I hate to sound like a broken record, but the political struggles and the billing issues are not avoided in this setting. Reimbursement is dependent upon the number of visits performed. Ten is the magic number for maximum payment, and the home health company managers will let you know about this number right off the bat. Most managers will tell you that they are here to treat the patient's needs and the ten-visit rule is not a requirement for therapists to meet. However, once you sign the dotted line and begin to treat patients, you may encounter a different theme. When you call in your frequency and duration, you may find that if it does not add up to ten or more visits it will be questioned. You may be asked to rethink your decision. You may even be questioned about missing something in your evaluation that you may be able to work on to achieve the ten visits. I discharged a patient before the tenth visit and the coordinator had the nerve to ask me if I had worked on safety education and a home exercise program. I felt like a kid being asked if I had cleaned my room and brushed my teeth. I felt like my professional ability was being challenged. I answered every question with a yes, and after a few more questions, I stopped her and explained that I could do no more for the patient and that was why I discharged her. I called a physical therapist friend of mine later that week and told him about the event. He told me he heard the same thing all the time. He came up with the perfect plan to stop the investigations into his judgments. He would respond with, "Are you asking me to commit Medicare fraud?" He said this question would end the conversation. He also said that after a few times asking that question they quit bothering him about the unwritten policy of the ten-visit rule. So if you find yourself in this situation, remember it is your ethical duty to report fraudulent behavior. Do not contribute to this practice. Treat the needs of the patient and do not let the managers get into your head. They will tell you about the bottom line, and some may tell you that Medicare wants everyone to be seen at least ten times. Do not fall for this lie. They will not stand up for you when the Medicare reviewers come calling, and I guarantee they will not have anything in their policies and procedures that say they encourage ten visits. You will have no supporting argument when you try to explain why you treated a patient eleven or twelve times, when six would have been sufficient. So a good idea would be to ask for the policy that requires at least ten visits when you are questioned about your frequency and duration or discharge decisions.

Discharges are tricky in any setting, but discharges in the home health political arena have to be within the top three most difficult. If you perform an evaluation and find no medical necessity to justify treating a patient, you may find it hard to discharge the patient without a little backlash from the physician or family member. You may even hear from the marketing or public relations officer. The physician could become unhappy because he or she wants the patient to have a certified nursing assistant go out three times a week and bathe the patient, and the only thing they could use to skill the patient was therapy. The family might be mad because now he or she will have to do it. The marketing officer might really be mad because he or she worked so hard trying to get that particular physician to refer patients and now that relationship is tarnished. Whatever reason they have for getting angry, you will be the one to hear about the problem first, and at that point you will have to make a decision to either stand by your word and professional ethics or cow tow and rewrite the evaluation to include a frequency and duration that will equal ten visits. Oh yeah. Don't forget that, if you decide to pick up the patient, you will then have to treat a person who does not need therapy for ten forty-five minutes sessions. Going into that house to sit and think of something to call skilled and trying to write the therapy note to reflect that will make your day seem like and eternity. Three times a week for four weeks is a long time, and at some point if you decide to do this injustice, I hope you feel your soul pulling at your heartstrings. If you do not feel your gut telling you something is wrong, then you can consider yourself sold-out and ethically bankrupt. If you find yourself justifying your actions with thoughts or statements like "no one will ever know" or "she really needs someone to bathe her," then know that you are in trouble. The all-time favorite justification is "the doctor ordered therapy, it must be done." This is the golden copout and it is used on a daily basis. If you check your state guidelines or the ethics section through the APTA, you will find that you are responsible for your actions—not the physician. If you knowingly treat a patient who has no potential for progress or does not meet the medical necessity guidelines, you are responsible for the repercussions.

The other single most important drawback to the home health setting deals with the term *homebound* and you can bet you will experience trouble with this issue. In order to be considered for home health services the patient must have a physical hardship that limits him or her from being able to leave their home. If they could leave home, an outpatient clinic would be the preferred method to deliver therapy services. Physical therapy goals are based on increasing the patient's physical independence, so juggling ten visits and trying to assist a person in regaining functional independence is tricky.

Patients are homebound when you begin therapy, but after six visits, they begin to improve significantly. Around the eighth visit, you find that you have to juggle your schedule around their trips to the mall. They are driving their cars and only need two or three visits to meet the unwritten ten-visit rule, do not forget about the grief you will get if you do not meet that goal. They may need a few more visits to complete the home exercise education goals, but they may no longer be homebound. Some patients have been told not to drive or go out of the house, because they would no longer be able to receive home health services. When this comment is made I am shocked, but I tell them that it is not true. I tell them that they can do anything they want to do, and I encourage them to get back to their former lifestyles. The goal of physical therapy is to have them back to their independent state. But if they can drive to the mall and shop, they do not qualify for home health services. I try to put this into perspective. I tell them in a round about way that everyone complains about Medicare fraud and abuse, except when they are involved and it benefits them.

STATE FACILITIES:
Mental Retardation/
Developmentally Delayed

POSITIVE

Working with the developmentally delayed client can be another challenging and rewarding experience in the career of a physical therapist. Most of the patients can be found in government-managed facilities and the funding typically comes from the state department of health and hospitals. I worked in a facility that cared for these patients, and the population was not comprised of children or adolescents like I had thought. The typical patient or client's age range fell between fifteen and seventy years old. This does not mean that all developmentally delayed settings will have this age range. I worked in this setting for approximately five years, and I do not regret a day of it. I had a chance to experience a challenge or two every day. I was able to get involved with the Special Olympics and work sports in as treatments for shoulder range of motion, strengthening, coordination, balance, and many other treatment-oriented activities. It was very exciting to be able to incorporate something fun into what could have been a mundane physical therapy plan of care. I used golf and bowling, horse shoes and baseball—anything fun and rewarding for the client. It motivated the client and in many cases the primary care giver. The diagnoses were typical childhood complications. The parents had abused some clients, resulting in brain injury and psychological disturbances. But typically the true developmental limitations were the majority of cases. Cerebral palsy, seizures, traumatic brain injury, and downs syndrome are just a few of the most common diagnoses you can expect to find. The term *client* is used for this population, and it is not the only term used. The term changes from patients to customer, from consumer to client, and it has changed again since then. I am not even sure what term is being used today, because it changes so much. The facilities are trying to get rid of the stigma that goes along with the term, but it has not worked in any facility I have been involved with. The factor to consider is human nature, and most people would like to soften the blow by changing what we call these people. But in my opinion they are humans and we should not try to change the terms we use. We should change the perceptions, or the stereotypical mindsets, in ourselves. They are humans in need of care and that is all that is important. Mental retardation is a fact not a slang term used to label a person in a bad light. Cancer is cancer and I do not see anyone trying to change it to a more subtle term. We usually just whisper it to soften the blow. That seems to work better than changing the name to "the process of cell mutation to an unhealthy state."

Off the soapbox and back to the positive. The state system is like any other state job, but I did not sit on my butt and look forward to retirement. I got involved with changing things and I ran into a great deal of resistance. It did not stop me, and I developed programs. Database management, statistics, staff training programs, performance improvement, quality assurance, environmental assessments, and staff safety programs are the primary areas I targeted. I am not trying to blow sunshine up my own skirt, but this gives you an idea of what you can do in this setting if you have the initiative. The individuals that you will have the privilege to work with in this setting will not be anything like patients in the other settings. Gait disturbances and balance issues will be coupled with behavioral and cognitive complications, and treatment will have to incorporate some training that you will not receive in PT school. It is difficult to treat a patient for a fall that had nothing to do with a gait or balance disturbance. I found myself becoming a damage-prevention consultant instead of a physical therapist. Whatever I could recommend to help prevent bodily harm in the form of assistance levels became the primary goal. Training staff to perform the assistance level correctly also became a valuable tool in injury prevention. Teaching direct care staff the art of transferring a dependent patient also proved to be an important role for our department. Mechanical lifts were an important piece of equipment in this setting, so get ready to use them if you go into this setting. Educating primary caregivers about positioning the patients, turn schedules, pressure-relief techniques, range of motion programs, fall prevention, ergonomics, back safety education, and many more techniques will be your primary function in this setting. It all depends on the acquity level (the amount of care the patient requires) of the patients assigned to your case-load. If you have the higher-level ambulatory patients or clients, you will not have the same treatment strategies as a peer who has the more dependent non-ambulatory clients. Overall, the care you will provide to these individuals will warm your heart, and seeing them smile as you come into the room is reward enough to come back day after day. The negative aspects can't compare with the feeling you will get daily from patient-care rewards.

NEGATIVE (REMEMBER THIS IS NOT THE CASE IN ALL STATE FACILITIES.)

Reimbursement in this setting is not an issue, except for finding enough money to provide for the patients needs. I can remember a time when our budget was so small we did not have toilet paper for our bathrooms. You can imagine what it was like trying to budget for equipment. The state is given a budget to work from, and that means you will not be asked to perform unethical acts to gain money from a private payer or Medicare. I am sure there are ways to find fraud in this setting but it is no comparison to any other sector. The drawbacks revolve around the political arena, the power struggle for territory, and most often the reluctance to change. For every good deed I performed, I experienced seven negative responses from my peers and other employees. Someone always has something to say about any decision you make or new program you implement. Ethical issues of state licensure laws can find their way into the mix but it is not as common in this setting. A pattern should be evolving in your mind at this point, because in every setting

I have mentioned, the difficulties and patient care practices have not been the primary hardship.

Staff retention in the primary caregiver arena was a very disheartening experience. The facility in which I worked had a training program that lasted just long enough for the new employee to reach the number of days to be eligible for unemployment. Employees would come in and go through the training program. They would work a couple of days in their assigned units, which involved direct supervision or on-the-job training, so they really did not work. Then they would not show up for work and or do something to be fired and, as a result, collect a check for unemployment. The pay was minimum wage and this had an impact on the type of person the job attracted. The work was not considered difficult or extremely demanding, but the actual client care is not for everyone. I think some of them just came to see what they considered to be a freak show. Being intrigued about the distorted bodies of the patients brought them in. The stories about the strange things that went on at night in the dorms spiked their interest. Once they got a glimpse of what they wanted to see, they left. And the turnover rate for primary caregivers stayed off the charts. How does all this relate to you? The primary caregivers in this setting are like the certified nursing assistants in the nursing home: you need them on a daily basis. If they do not care about doing a good job, then it makes your job harder. If the facility is short staffed, it makes your job harder. One day you will understand what I am talking about when you try to implement a range of motion or positioning program. If you truly care about the patient, you will find it difficult to ask a minimum wage employee who is over-worked due to staff shortages to perform extra duties to help you meet your goals for the patient. These employees will be more concerned with hygiene care and feeding than ROM or positioning, and in most cases they do not care about the proper way to handle a patient in terms of mobility. They are looking for the fastest way to get the patient from point A to point B, and a mechanical lift is not fast in their opinion. They would rather risk their backs and the patients safety to hurry up and get to the next bath or feeding.

No one asked me to do anything except evaluate and treat patients in this setting, but I took the bull by the horns and built a database. We needed to be able to track our services. I soon began gathering statistics that would enable us to see the overall picture of what the department did to contribute to the livelihood of the individuals we cared for. I did not have any formal training in Microsoft Access, so I enlisted some help and soon got the hang of it. Once it was complete and the information was entered, I ran queries. To my amazement, patterns began to develop and I gained an incredible amount of insight about our contribution to this facility. It was not long before it became evident that we were not providing the significantly compromised individuals with enough formal hands-on treatments. This was primarily due to inadequate training. Most, if not all, of the PT staff came from settings that dealt with typical patients and typical problems. They gained knowledge from experiences in outpatient or acute care settings and nursing homes. No one had a good basic knowledge of developmentally delayed individuals. Because of this problem, most of the individuals who received treatment were picked up because the therapist had an idea of what to do to help solve the problem.

The other more debilitated individuals were passed over based on cognitive issues and an overall poor prognosis for return of function. To top it off, the evaluation did not paint a picture of why the services were deemed inappropriate. I began running one query after another, and before long I realized the problem with our treatment philosophy. We were not treating the most life-threatening issues due to lack of proper training.

I have included letters and memos in this book to show you real events and real situations. This will give you an account of what really goes on in the world of PT.

Note: *These letters were written to the new administrator of our department. We went through several in a four- or five-year period.*

Jane,

I began thinking of a possible solution to finding the appropriate candidates for direct PT intervention while going through the diagnosis query looking for correlations between people on active treatment as it relates to the diagnosis. I came across an evaluation of an individual on active treatment (aquatic therapy). The individual had the following diagnoses/limitations.

Spastic Quadriplegia
Contractures
Dependent Mobility
CVA, OA, HTN, Reflux,

The treatment focus revolved around strengthening, weight bearing, and relaxation activities. The body of the summary did not give a reason for the treatments performed in relation to diagnoses. Nor did it state how the treatment will assist this individual in achieving personal goals.

I immediately thought of an individual who I observed just recently. I imagined that she was my daughter, and I began to wonder why my daughter was not on some kind of active treatment program, because she is totally dependent with every aspect of mobility and cannot hold her head in the correct position to swallow effectively. If I visited the PT department and observed higher-level individuals receiving care, I would want to know why the PT department is working with someone who can move about with assistance and drive an electric wheelchair instead of my daughter. I would assume that nothing could be done to help my child and I would want to know why. If we are stating that an individual is not a candidate for direct PT intervention. We should explain why.

I soon realized that if I could come up with a prioritized list of diagnoses that are most detrimental to the human body, I could find patients with the highest priority for direct PT intervention (hands-on therapy). I decided to begin with the most important bodily processes needed to sustain life. Assuming the heart is in good condition, the primary functions are oxygen delivery, nutrition, skin integrity, and waste elimination. Is the PT department directly involved (hands-on treatment) with the basic functions of the human body? What does a physical therapist do in order to improve an individual with one or all of the primary systems compromised?

1. Respiration: What compromises it? Significant abnormal spinal curvatures and aspiration influence the respiratory system. What can cause it? Poor posture (scoliosis) and or improper head positioning. Assuming speech therapy could not resolve the aspiration or swallowing problem with therapeutic intervention, how do we assist? Cervical musculature strengthening/ coordination/ decrease tone → improved posture and head control to provide the proper posture. How do we assist regarding spinal

curvatures? Some time ago, one of our staff members went to a training course here on campus. The training dealt with improving the O2 sat levels by increasing the lung capacity. The presenter demonstrated, placing an individual with a significant scoliosis across her lap (side lying with the convex portion of the curve inferior). She was able to decrease spinal curvatures, improving O2 sat levels instantly.

Present hands on PT intervention (unknown, no supportive documentation)
Indirect intervention- Physical Support, training

Indirect intervention- PT provides a written plan of care (physical support) for the direct care staff to follow in regards to patient care. The therapist formally trains the direct care staff and they are responsible for correctly handling, positioning, and feeding the patient.

2. Nutrition- What compromises it? Swallowing complications, Aspiration, poor posture, how do we assist? Strength/balance training for the trunk/cervical musculature → proper positioning. Strength/coordination training for the UE musculature → increased independent feeding.

    Present hands on PT intervention- (Unknown, no supportive documentation)
    Indirect intervention- Physical Support, training.

3. Skin Integrity- What compromises it? Circulatory compromise, improper positioning, decreased mobility, poor nutrition, how do we assist? Improve circulation via active muscle contraction, strength/ bed mobility training, etc. Right here I see the domino affect coming into focus, we are not providing treatment for the most life threatening issues.

   Present hands on PT intervention- (Unknown, no supportive documentation)
   Indirect intervention- Physical Support, training.

4. Waste elimination: What compromises it? Decreased mobility, decreased upright positioning, how do we assist? Increase strength → increase mobility → increase upright positioning.

   Present hands on PT intervention- (None)-Unless we are performing treatment sessions and documenting that PT is directly affecting the function with physical activity and proper upright positioning.

   Indirect intervention- Unknown- unless we are documenting "positioning is facilitating the individuals digestive track by providing the appropriate bowel elimination positions."

I know all of this seems simple, but if we work off the primary bodily functions, we can be sure that we are not missing the individuals who are the most vulnerable. Currently, the documentation proves that we are concerned; however, it depicts an indirect approach via the physical support and staff training. We are not providing specific treatments that target these life threatening issues, nor are we addressing them in our documenting.

The next thought that comes to mind is the variety of cognitive levels we will come across. Most patients are unable to participate secondary to cognitive limitations; they should be the primary candidates for PT intervention. The cognitive limitations should not limit our ability to treat the patient. PROM and relaxation techniques could assist an individual with increased tone to attain the proper position for swallowing food and could be performed without the individual's mental participation. Once we figure out what we do and how we do it, I am sure the rest will become very clear. If we start with the basic life-sustaining function and branch out from there, looking at all the diagnoses that affect it directly, we can begin to prioritize without thinking. What is the diagnosis and how does it compromise breathing, eating, bowel, bladder and skin integrity?

I hope this helps,

Monie Phillips PT

Jane,

I thought of something that I feel we may not be looking deeply into with this population: developmental reflexes. We are not tracking them at all, and I am almost positive we are not addressing them as our primary concern or incorporating them into the treatment plans or physical support. As you know, the way we were taught to work with individuals diagnosed with MRDD depended primarily upon the reflexes that have not integrated. I have a book at home, and I will be glad to bring it in if you do not have access to this type of literature. I am thinking that to become a developmental center PT department we should be concentrating on the pathological reflexes and basing our treatment plans on them. Most of us have not been trained extensively in this area, and we bring what we know from our accumulative PT experiences and apply that the best we can with this population. I am not sure if anyone here has had any experience with this population before working here. I know this sounds crazy, but that may be why we did not see extensive documentation and appropriate treatment strategies. Let me know what you think and if you would like the book. The OT director let me borrow some videotapes some time ago that dealt with positioning according to diagnosis, and I realized then that if I had a case load of patients with 95 to 100 percent severe mental retardation I would feel as if I were neglecting them secondary to my limited knowledge of and experience with this population. I have had a large number of patients and I know I felt overwhelmed. I worked with the immediate problems at hand that usually revolved around handling the individual or the physical support. I did not have the time to stop and look into the developmental reflexes, much less attempt to begin a rehab program to stimulate the individual into reflex integration. I began looking for help, looking into centers around the world on the Internet. I found a lot of different techniques and only a few centers devoted to programs, research, and development. One that astonished me had a very high success rate but a reputation of using radical techniques. During my search I also learned that the success rate largely depended upon early intervention. This is the reason for the continuing education courses that only deal with the pediatric population. I have not seen any that deal with geriatric or adult MRDD.

Monie

SALARY

Now we get to the part you are anxious to hear about. The average salary of a licensed physical therapist has been calculated across the nation, and I am here to tell you the numbers are not completely right. I searched for salary ranges on several different Web sites and came up with a very different number than what we are used to in my area. The site listed for my area $50,000 a year as the low and $58,000 as the high. Now I know this statistic is wrong, because I live here and I know what the salary range is to be competitive. The factor that plays a big role in the salary determination is simple supply and demand. When a town becomes saturated with therapists the demand goes down and the salary goes right with it. The states that attract therapists pay less because a high volume of therapists want to live in the area. For instance, Colorado is a great skiing and vacation area, and the state has very little trouble finding people who want to live and work there. The cost of living is extremely high and the pay for therapists is extremely low when compared to less attractive states.

SETTINGS AND SALARIES

Home health companies are known to pay a greater amount than any other setting for staff therapists. They usually pay by the visit, and they do pay for mileage. Thirty-five to forty-five dollars a visit and thirty cents a mile is about average. If you are paid by the visit, the patient census will be a factor that determines your annual income. If your visits go down because the agency is experiencing low patient volume, you will not be paid for sitting around the office waiting for patient referrals.

Owning an outpatient clinic is another way to increase your earning potential, but make sure you have business experience. The billing issues and politics can bring you to your knees if you are not prepared. Your yearly salary can reach $100,000 and up, but be prepared to work for every penny.

Veteran's affairs and state or government jobs are typically the lowest paying jobs on the market today, but you may find one of these agencies paying more because they are in a bind. This could mean they are having internal problems, so watch out. The typical starting pay is $45,000 to $55,000 a year, and you can look forward to the yearly cost-of-living raises.

Hospitals and rehabilitation hospitals average about the same salary range. On an average, $50,000 to $60,000 a year is a good estimate for these settings.

I cannot comment on physical therapy salaries in the professional sports setting because I have never experienced anything firsthand. I have heard that $90,000 to $100,000 a year is possible.

Experience is a factor in most staff positions but remember supply and demand is the greatest contributing factor.

Administrative positions can pay up to $78,000 a year, depending on the geographical location. Again, it all depends on the supply and demand in the area.

OUTPATIENT SETTING INTERVIEW QUESTIONS

What is the primary referral base?
- Accident/injury
- Workers' compensation
- Orthopedic
- Other

If it is determined that additional equipment is needed, will the clinic support the need?

Does the clinic support an athletic program? Will I be allowed, encouraged, or expected to participate in the program?

If the primary therapist calls in sick or takes an extended vacation, will I be expected to take the excess patient load?

Does the clinic currently have additional PRN staff members to handle volume overload?

If a physician calls in an order for therapy, who takes the order?

Will I be given an opportunity to consult with a therapist who has more experience if at any time I feel uncertain when determining a treatment decision or if I have questions regarding patient care issues?

ACUTE CARE INTERVIEW QUESTIONS

Who has the responsibility of keeping up with the Medicare changes and billing procedures?

What is the expected productivity for each therapist?

Is the director responsible for any other disciplines? Is the rehab director a therapist? If so, what discipline?

When is the next JCAHO visit and what is the hospital doing to prepare for that visit?

What is the long-range plan for the hospital and the PT department?

Do you currently have a good line of communication with the referring physicians, nurses, case managers, and social workers?

Do you currently have discharge planning sessions or meetings with utilization review and does the treating PT have enough time during the day to attend the meetings?

Does the hospital currently employ a majority of RN's or LPN's?

Does the hospital have a patient care advocate or representative?

Is the hospital driven by patient satisfaction and is a tracking system currently in place?

Has the hospital updated to computer charting?

What is the process regarding discharge summaries?

NURSING HOME INTERVIEW QUESTIONS

What productivity level will be expected and what repercussions will be taken if the level is not produced due to low census or unforeseen complications?

Does the MDS coordinator work well with the rehab manager?

What qualifications does the MDS coordinator have regarding Medicare regulations?

Does the MDS coordinator stay abreast of the daily changes regarding SNF Medicare rules and regulations? If so, how?

Does the nursing home have Internet access, and can the therapy staff members access it for Medicare research purposes?

Does the nursing home have a restorative program?

Will there be any traveling? Will I have to work in other nursing homes?

Will I have to work weekends to make up missed minutes during the week?

Does the rehab management company put pressure on the therapists to achieve ultra-high RUG's?

HOME HEALTH INTERVIEW QUESTIONS

Does the home health agency discharge a patient if he/she does not meet medical necessity and homebound status? What is the policy on the issue?

Does the home health agency pressure therapists to provide a minimum of ten visits regardless of the patients needs? Is there a policy to help prevent this type of pressure?

If a staff member attempts to persuade a therapist to meet the ten-visit minimum, what recourse does the therapist have?

Will the payment be per visit or a salary?

If pay-per-visit is selected, what is the minimum number of visits per week that is considered full time?

If the salary position is chosen, what will be the maximum number of visits expected? If the maximum number is exceeded on a regular basis, what process will be utilized to remedy the situation?

What will be expected if the census decreases?

Will the agency provide blood pressure cuffs, oxygen saturation monitors, gait belts, and other necessary treatment equipment or is the therapist responsible for providing the items?

If a patient complains about nursing services, the therapist shall report the incident to whom?

If a family member or patient complains about a therapist's decision to discharge the patient due to non-homebound reasons or the lack of participation on the patient's part, will the agency support the decision of the therapist?

STANDARD INTERVIEW QUESTIONS

What does the job entail as far as duties and responsibilities?

Who do I report to and who will be rating my performance?

How many patients will I be expected to see a day?

What is the average length of time allotted to treat patients?

How much time is allotted for documentation and nonproductive activities?

What will be expected when and if the census drops?

How many therapists currently work in the clinic, and how many years of experience do they have?

Will I have a mentor?

If I objectively determine that a patient is not a candidate for skilled therapy services and discharged them against a physician's recommendation, would the clinic support the decision?

Does the job entail any additional duties?

Does the clinic allow technicians to perform modalities and treatments?

Are professional dues and continuing education paid for by the company and are therapists encouraged to specialize?

Will I be expected to work weekends or be on call?

What is the current policy regarding overtime?

Will I be responsible for PTA supervision?

Does the department currently have programs in place to prevent fraud and abuse?

Does the department have a no retaliation policy?

Does the department encourage creative thinking?

What types of advancement opportunities are available?

CONCLUSION

The book was not written to be a deterrent to those desiring to enter the physical therapy profession. It is not intended to shed a bad light on those who are practicing today. It is designed to help improve your decision-making process. This book has discussed what it takes to get in and what type of person the field needs to help promote the profession in a positive light. We discussed the physical therapy program, and we have discussed salary potential. We have also discussed the issues that you may be exposed to once you begin practicing, issues you might already be facing today. I realize that some of the things you have read may have burdened your heart and that the negative parts of the book might have hit a cord. This book was not written to improve the physical therapy candidate numbers. Nor was it designed to be a deterrent. It was written to provide a true account of the profession for people who are thinking about going into the field and people who have graduated from a physical therapy program and are ready to begin practicing. The book is also written for the many physical therapists practicing today. I hope this information has helped you feel that this is a great profession and there is hope for the future. I anticipate that the physical therapy world will take the information that is now public knowledge and heed the warnings that are laced throughout this book; we must take a stand and protect the dignity of our profession. Providing ambulation training for a patient with a primary diagnosis of a urinary tract infection with no signs of gait or balance disturbances has to stop along with all the other non-skilled services. The public is watching every move we make, and the information superhighway is providing everyone with more education regarding fraud and improper practices. If we are not careful, the field will one day be looked upon with skepticism, and the need for our services will fade in the eyes of the public. As the compression of morbidity draws near, the need for increased cost savings for Medicare recipients will be increasingly scrutinized by government agencies. If you are currently contributing to or plan to contribute to this ever-present problem, know that it is going to come around and bite you one day. It will bite all of us if we do not stop the current management philosophies and strategies designed to maximize revenue without regard to medical necessity or physical therapy practice guidelines and ethics issues. Please, for the sake of this country and our profession, take a stand against fraud and abuse. Risk everything to protect your dignity and the dignity of our profession. I can promise you one thing: You will feel better about standing up for yourself to begin with. It will get rid of that nasty feeling in your stomach. If you find yourself in need of assistance because the agency or someone in the agency is retaliating or threatening you or your job because you chose to stand up for what is right, contact your local physical therapy board or the staff member in your agency responsible for compliance. If you ever feel like you are being pressured to perform unethical acts to improve revenue or gain the favor of physicians or patients, report the issue immediately. Once you set the standard by looking the other way or complying with this behavior, you will find it hard to refute it the next time.

The field of physical therapy is a great profession. It is very rewarding and the patients are great. Helping people return to their lives with less pain, more strength, education, healed wounds, normal gait patterns, and all of the other areas the profession addresses will last a lifetime. It is the gift that keeps on giving, and many patients will never forget your efforts. If you are currently working in the field, do not give up hope. If you are thinking of joining the profession, do so with all of your might. If you are a new graduate and you are looking for a facility or clinic to join, make sure the philosophy of the establishment revolves around patient care and a sound work ethic. Whatever we do, we must follow the truth, and I am praying that this book has helped you make a decision in your life that will last a lifetime.

I trust the information provided in this book will serve as a catalyst to help promote in a positive light the physical therapy profession and help you, the reader, better understand and hone interviewing skills and on-the-job skills as you seek employment and as you execute your professional responsibilities.

Truthfully,

Monie Phillips PT

ABOUT THE AUTHOR

MONIE PHILLIPS is a licensed Physical Therapist in the state of Louisiana practicing in an acute care setting as the Director of Rehab services. Monie served a total of ten years in the Air Force as a Jet Engine Mechanic, he is licensed as an Airframe and Powerplant mechanic and he worked for the Jackson International Airport as Chief Inspector while finishing his prerequisite course work for Physical Therapy. Monie served in the Mississippi Air Nation Guard during the Gulf War and later resigned his positions in the Aircraft industry completely when he was accepted into the Physical Therapy program. He graduated form the University of Mississippi Medical Center in May of 1996. Monie was born in Jackson Mississippi were he met and married his wife Candace who is a Registered Nurse / Branch manager in a Home Health setting. They have three healthy children, two girls and a boy, Presley, Kelsie and Monie IV. Monie and Candace are devoted to God, family and profession. Monie enjoys weight training, wakeboarding, Jet Skiing, and helping others.

Made in the USA
Lexington, KY
24 December 2009